Improving Children's Services Networks

Improving Children's Services Networks

Lessons from Family Centres

Jane Tunstill,
Jane Aldgate and
Marilyn Hughes

Jessica Kingsley Publishers
London and Philadelphia

First published in 2007
by Jessica Kingsley Publishers
116 Pentonville Road
London N1 9JB, UK
and
400 Market Street, Suite 400
Philadelphia, PA 19106, USA

www.jkp.com

Library of Congress Cataloging in Publication Data
A CIP catalog record for this book is available from the Library of Congress

British Library Cataloguing in Publication Data
A CIP catalogue record for this book is available from the British Library

ISBN-13: 978 1 84310 461 2
ISBN-10: 1 84310 461 X

Printed and bound in Great Britain by
Athenaeum Press, Gateshead, Tyne and Wear

Contents

List of Tables

Acknowledgements

This book owes its inspiration and existence to the families and the staff in family centres who generously gave of their time and expertise throughout its design and execution. Without them there would have been no study, and we hope we have done justice to their vision of what family centres can achieve. We were especially grateful to both parents and staff who generously agreed to their views being quoted, on the basis that we safeguarded their anonymity. The Family Centre Network and National Council of Voluntary Child Care Organisations welcomed and provided us with a unique opportunity to explore the experiences of their members. Ian Vallender and Erica D'Eath deserve our special thanks. We are also indebted to Moraene Roberts and her colleagues at ATD Fourth World for their wisdom and generosity.

There were many other individuals who supported us including those in the children's services world on whose ideas and expertise we have drawn. In particular we would like to thank the following: James Blewett, Co-ordinator, Making Research Count, King's College, London; Lesley-Anne Cull, Dean, Faculty of Health and Social Care, The Open University; Rupert Hughes, CBE; Mark Peel; Wendy Rose, Senior Research Fellow, The Open University; Janet Seden, Senior Lecturer, The Open University; Professor June Thoburn, Professor Emeritus, University of East Anglia.

Finally we would like to thank, for their painstaking and meticulous administrative support, not to mention their endless patience, Shirley Chambers and Agnes McGill.

Jane Tunstill
Jane Aldgate
Marilyn Hughes

Chapter 1

An Introduction to the Study

In many ways, the story of family centres in the last quarter of the twentieth century provides a microcosm of the overall development of child care policy and practice and reflects many of the current emphases of national government policies. In particular, family centres provide an example of the potential of centre-based services, which strive to provide a wide range of services within local communities. In addition, the fact that family centres have been provided by both statutory and voluntary sector agencies reflects the long-standing emphasis of governments, including the present one, on partnership working across sectors. Family centres have also had a history of working closely in an interdisciplinary context. The literature on family centres might, therefore, be seen as a useful resource for current policy initiatives on children's services. In short, as this book will show, family centres themselves can play a key role in contributing to positive outcomes for children, their families and the communities in which they live. In fact, the knowledge base around their organization and operation has much to offer the development of children's services in line with the requirements of *Every Child Matters* (CM 5860, 2003).

Family centres and building knowledge

The insight provided into the work of family centres is fundamental to the current aspirations of government for children's services, including children's trusts, children's centres, and extended schools. All the new 'structures' face many of the same challenges which have traditionally faced family centres, for example, working with a range of partners; addressing family support *and* child protection; facilitating access to services. Over and above this, family centres have a role to play in meeting the needs of local communities, and where appropriate, increasing social capital.

As we can see from the emphasis on the evaluation as well as the achievement of outcomes for children, policy is now increasingly intended to be evidence based. Although at face value, a self-evidently good and practical notion, in reality there is a robust literature as to what policy makers, researchers, practitioners, and those who use services actually mean by the concept of 'What works?' (Sanderson 2002; Solesbury 2001). In addition, questions have been raised as to the feasibility of proving beyond all doubt what strategies do and do not work (Coote *et al.* 2004; Auspos and Kubisch 2004).

Our study, while not measuring the level of outcomes for individual children, has collected data on a wide range of activity in family centres. Much of this is relevant to children's centres. Our findings include topics of current importance, such as:

- the management of partnerships

- meeting the needs of a diverse community

- the impact of workforce issues

- engaging service-users.

We would point to the helpfulness of Pawson's view (Pawson 2004) that there is a need for a new and more realistic approach to the evaluation of programmes and/or services. Although his arguments have been made in the context of complex community initiatives, they also apply both to the nature and the potential application to policy, of some of our own data. He argues for prioritizing some programme components above others, on the grounds that it is better to draw out and test thoroughly a limited number of really key programme theories, than to try and achieve an approximate sketch of it all.

Our study contains insights into aspects of programme components that are likely to have relevance beyond the family centre system *per se*. These issues include:

- access to services

- partnership working

- co-ordination of services

- multi-agency working

- networking.

The findings from this study of family centres have the potential to contribute to the building of knowledge about community-based services for children and families. We believe that such an approach, based on an explicit acknowledgement of the value of such knowledge building, can be very helpful to policy makers and practitioners in that it provides a range of insights from different vantage points. It is not always necessary to reinvent the wheel in order to build knowledge. The experiences of family centres can be used to take forward the agenda of the Children Act 2004 across a range of agencies and projects, including children's centres. To that end, we have identified from our study findings a set of messages for the current children's services agenda. Therefore,

Chapters 3 to 8 identify a set of messages for the current children's services agenda at the end of each chapter.

However, before proceeding to describe the contemporary framework within which family centres now operate, it is essential to provide a brief overview of their evolution, rationale and characteristics. Their diversity, in many ways a strength, has sometimes, ironically and indeed, perversely, appeared to contribute to a lack of understanding about their scope and purpose.

What are family centres?

It is notoriously difficult to produce the definitive description of a family centre. Early literature on family centres, including their potential for linking families with other agencies in the way perceived by the Audit Commission (1994), was largely descriptive (for example, Warren 1993; Smith 1996), and often concerned with the elucidation of models or categories of family centres. An early model suggested three categories of family centre:

- client-focused centres associated with professional, specialized, therapeutic, statutory work with referred clients

- neighbourhood-focused centres, often located in areas of high social need, combining targeted, direct services with open access to a range of activities, with an emphasis on participation and voluntary activity, within a neighbourhood or community setting

- community development oriented centres less involved in traditional, direct social work than in the promotion of self help and empowerment of communities, having a support and liaison role and providing premises for other groups and services (Holman 1987).

Later, Cannan (1992) added a fourth type to this model: 'service centre' to meet a range of day care needs, not restricted to health or social problems. Warren (1993) further developed the categorization of family centres to cover:

- family support centres

- community development centres

- integrated centres, combining referred and drop in facilities

- parent-craft centres

- day care plus other services

- assessment and treatment for referred families

- creative residential centres providing short-term care for adolescents.

In addition to such categorization, early studies of individual family centres demonstrated a number of common themes with an emphasis on: prevention of child abuse, reception into care and family breakdown (for example, Adamson 1987; Atherton 1987); community work (for example, Hasler 1984; Holman 1987; Cigno 1988; Heaton and Sayer 1992); the problem of stigma (for example, Cannan 1986); networking (Cox *et al.* 1992); partnership (for example, Eisenstadt 1983; Daines 1989); and differences in philosophy, such as a focus on families' strengths or dysfunctional aspects (Department of Health and Social Security, Social Services Inspectorate 1988; Cannan 1992).

In the late 1980s and early 1990s, it was noted that although family centres could have a common approach or philosophy, in reality they could vary considerably in their practice. The Family Centre Network (having a membership of around 450 centres from both the statutory and voluntary sectors) in 1987 defined family centres as being 'shorthand' for an approach that brings together those who subscribe to an holistic approach to families, with the emphasis on the organization of services in the locality and maximum participation of consumers (National Family Centre Network 1987). In terms of family centre operation and activity, there were always likely to be multiple influences. Holman argues that, given that such influences included the continual process of negotiation which takes place between professions (and different segments of each profession) and their wider organizations, such as the role of management and wider leadership and local politics, one could not expect centres to settle into fixed types or that certain types of organization (social services departments, community groups) would run centres of a certain type (Holman 1988).

Holman's view serves to underline the dynamic nature of family centres, which has always enabled them to be responsive to change. Two recently published sets of findings underline this characteristic, and highlight their continuing relevance to the implementation of current policy agendas. Firstly, as Ranson and Rutledge (2005) conclude, family centres represent important community resources, which are capable of providing local support to parents and children, and constitute a key potential resource for government policies that target families in deprived areas. They have the potential to influence change in individuals, families and communities, in which latter role they can help transform the culture of public services to one of knowledge exchange rather than transmission, and to partnership rather than public deference to professional power. Similarly, a study undertaken in Scotland (Tisdall *et al.* 2005) explored the integration of children's services in Scotland in the context of family centres and new Community Schools. They found that parents valued both the 'one stop shop' provided by family centres, as well as the continuity they provided in services and relationships. In addition to providing support themselves, these relationships could act as conduits into other agencies and services. There could sometimes be a shortfall in anticipated benefits, when family problems were particularly complex, and/or where the inter-agency team was inhibited by geographical or resource boundaries. Unsurprisingly, short-term funding and staff shortages could limit the potential for successfully integrating the services.

Both these studies capture the challenges of delivering the *Every Child Matters* agenda (CM 5860, 2003) and, at the same time, highlight the vital role that family centres can play in the expanding service networks which are antici-pated in the Children Act 2004.

Our own study findings point in the same overall direction and, in this book, we explore their relevance for the task of creating and sustaining those service networks. We hope to show that family centres are in a pivotal position to contribute to the new agenda, including the development of children's trusts and children's centres.

Overview of the book

This study is one of the 11 studies commissioned in 1994 to be undertaken over several years, within the *Supporting Parents* Initiative funded by the Depart-ment of Health. This study was the last to start. These studies, along with three others funded as commissioned studies by the Department of Health, are described in the overview of the *Supporting Parents* Initiative (Quinton 2004). All of the studies reported within this overview contain important messages for current policy development.

Quinton identifies a set of four cross-cutting themes which he explores under the following headings:

- concepts of support and parenting

- informal support

- support and services

- inter-agency working (Quinton 2004, p.6).

The findings from our own study constitute one of the strands in these themes. While our own primary focus was very obviously on the subject of inter-agency working, some of the other overview messages for policy and practice which Quinton identifies have a very obvious link with the aims and activities of family centres. These include the following:

- In modern societies parenting is complex and hard to do.

- Parenting – what parents do with their children – arises from many influences.

- The ecological perspective points up the complexity between these influences and formal services are part of this ecology.

- All parents wanted to feel in control in dealing with parenting problems.

- Parents should first be seen as experts in their own parenting even when their views may need to be changed.

- Support is a relationship that requires respect and partnership.

- Support is also a process – services need to get off on the right foot and be aware of and responsive to changing needs (see Quinton 2004).

This book makes its major contribution to the *Supporting Parents* Initiative by showing the central contribution of family centres to the task of supporting parents in the community and by exploring the challenges of inter-agency working. Given the perennial, and indeed highly topical, significance of both these subjects, wherever possible, we have made links between our data and the current children's services agenda.

Aims and design of the study

The overall objective and starting point for the study was to explore the potential of the Audit Commission proposal in 1994 that family centres could function as a major access route to a range of family support services for parents. A large number of family centres were (and indeed still are) members of the Family Support Network, based at National Council for Voluntary Child Care Organisations. This umbrella group was very supportive of the study intentions, and facilitated access to the Network membership; without such enthusiastic participation on the part of the centres, our findings would have been far less illuminating and multi-dimensional.

The aims of the study therefore were as follows:

- to examine the potential of family centres to act as a gateway to family support services

- to explore the extent to which family centres facilitate or develop links with informal support networks within the community

- to identify the potential for family centres to act as co-ordinating centres for family support services.

There were three main phases to the study:

- The national survey: a postal survey of an extensive sample of 559 family centres in England, drawn from the Family Centre Network membership, of whom 415 took part in the study.

- The intensive study: an in-depth study of a purposive sample of 40 of these family centres, selected from the extensive sample in order to examine, in more detail, specific aspects of family centre work. This phase used face-to-face interviews with key stakeholders.

- The review survey: a follow-up by postal survey questionnaire, of respondents in the extensive sample. Out of a possible 408 still in business, 344 centres took part. The review took place in order to ensure optimum policy currency, given the fast rate of policy change in this period. It provided an opportunity to capture the changes in train and their impact on family centre activity.

- Parents' perspectives: in addition, at the first phase, 83 parents from 28 centres were interviewed.

For more detail, see the Appendix.

The structure of the book

This chapter has provided an introduction to the subject of family centres and outlined the aims of the study which is at the heart of the book. Chapter 2 provides the contemporary policy context. In Chapters 3 to 9, the main findings of the study are presented. At the end of Chapters 3 to 8, we outline the relevance of the findings for the current children's policy agenda. Chapter 9 describes family centres in transition. We then add an afterword to locate family centres in the current policy developments. At the end of the book, there is an Appendix, in which the study's methodology is described. The chapters may be summarized as follows.

Chapter 2: The Current Agenda for Children and Family Services

This chapter establishes an up-to-date policy context for the book by providing an overview of the key developments since 1997 in community level services for children and families. It outlines the relationship between the Children Act 1989 *Every Child Matters* (CM 5860, 2003) and the Children Act 2004 and highlights the potential usefulness of our data on family centres for those policy makers and practitioners who will be responsible for implementing the changes required. These include the establishment of children's centres, as required by the National Child Care Strategy (HM Treasury 2004).

Chapter 3: Building Links and Partnerships with Other Agencies

This chapter describes the ways in which family centres build and sustain networks with other agencies. It includes findings on both formal and informal links. The chapter underlines the importance of having an explicit commitment to partnership at the heart of the formal policies of centre-based provision in the community. This has always been traditionally true of family centres and is likely to apply just as strongly to children's centres in the future. Making this commitment explicit gives a very clear message to other agencies about the value of partnership. In the light of any anxieties or misapprehensions that local stakeholders may hold about the likely impact of children's centres on their work, this will be even more crucial.

Chapter 4: Family Centres and Social Services: Tensions and Opportunities

This chapter looks at the relationship between family centres and social services in some depth. It explores the factors that foster or hinder good communication between the two. It also shows how social services and family centres can have a mutually beneficial partnership in spite of the barriers that sometimes inhibit their relationship.

Chapter 5: Delivering Services: The Experience of Family Centres

The chapter presents an overview of the services on offer in family centres, including the range of routes to access services within the centre. It describes the various combinations of services which can be provided to meet the needs of parents and their children. The chapter also explores the implications of the way in which services are delivered. In particular it highlights the balance between early and late intervention services, a tension which, in some cases, can change the role of the centre from a preventive to a reactive one.

Chapter 6: Centres as a Gateway to Other Services: The Experience of Family Centres

This chapter shows the valuable role that family centres can play in organizing a wide range of children's services. It describes how centre staff co-operate with each other and other professionals across health and social care to provide an integrated service for children and families. It highlights how family centres play a creative and innovative role in developing the social skills of parents through groupwork and networking with other adults and children.

This chapter shows that the ability of family centres to offer a range of services depends on the level of sophistication of different networks. The chapter is innovative in that it shows how complex the range of networking models can be. For example networks can include links between agencies; some are established because of existing funding arrangements; and others derive from the pressure of referrals from statutory services. In addition family centres have a key role in contributing to the implementation of government initiatives such as Sure Start.

Chapter 7: The Importance of Centre Managers and Staff

This chapter focuses on the people who work in family centres. It shows that the majority of family centre staff are female; and that there is an under-representation of black and minority ethnic workers. The chapter explores the importance of continuing professional development and access to training in order to develop a competent workforce. Workers can comprise a source of mutual support for each other which can in turn, enhance their respective potential for making a positive contribution to the lives of children in the community.

Chapter 8: Parents' Perspectives on Family Centres

In this chapter we discuss the impact of parental participation in decision making on the work of the centre. The chapter shows how family centres can be an important source of empowerment for parents by encouraging their active participation. The study shows how parents appreciate their relationships with staff as well as their interactions with other parents. It also underlines the fact that support services need to recognize that parents are experts on their own strengths and needs. A parent-led approach to services needs to be built into service delivery, whether those services are open access with parents referring themselves, or are triggered by referrals from professionals.

Chapter 9: Family Centres in Transition

This chapter highlights the perennial and considerable stress which is generated by policy change for those who deliver services. This rate of change has an impact on both the work and the organization of family centres. By identifying individual policy phases, the chapter shows how family centres have increased support services for children, including out-of-school activities. Children's centres are only the most recent manifestation of this change. The chapter shows overwhelming evidence that family centres have a major and positive impact on support services for vulnerable families, and have the capacity to act as a 'one stop shop'. This should leave them in a pivotal position in the new services configuration.

Family Centres: An Afterword

The book concludes by emphasizing the case that has been made throughout, that family centres should occupy a pivotal position in any new services configuration. In particular, we conclude that they have important lessons to offer policy makers and practitioners as they implement the *Every Child Matters* agenda. These lessons, if taken on board by policy makers and practitioners, could make a very substantial and positive contribution to the process of developing children's centres.

Chapter 2

The Current Agenda for Children and Family Services

This chapter sets out the policy context within which family centres have been operating and evolving, over the course of the last twenty years or so, up until the time of writing in 2006. This period incorporates an unusually high degree of change in the organization of services for families and coincided with the beginning of the present decade when the first fieldwork for this study began to be undertaken. This policy account is necessarily selective, given the scale of the political, organizational and professional changes involved, and can only hope to highlight the key features of the policy framework within which family centres have developed in this period. The policy imperatives outlined in this chapter include two important pieces of child welfare legislation, the Children Act 1989 and the Children Act 2004. Taken together they have both determined the scope that family centres possess to address any of the issues raised by our study data. At the same time, they have inevitably raised new implementation challenges in their own right.

We have organized this policy account into three sections:

1. The relationship between family centres and the Children Act 1989.

2. Changing policy developments between 1997 and 2003 which have had a major impact on family centres.

3. The policy implications of *Every Child Matters* and the Children Act 2004.

The relationship between family centres and the Children Act 1989

The Children Act 1989 remains the primary legislation in England and Wales in relation to services for safeguarding and promoting the welfare of children. The Children Act 2004, described in more detail below, strengthens co-operation between agencies to safeguard and promote the welfare of children but does not change the importance of Section 17 of the Children Act 1989, with its mandate for family support services.

Family centres were an important component in the family support philosophy of the Children Act 1989 and indeed were the only individual service to be specified within the Act. When examined in the context of the Act overall, it is easy to see their currency:

> The definition of need is deliberately wide to reinforce the emphasis on preventive support to families. It has three categories: a reasonable standard of health or development; significant impairment of health or development; and disablement. (Department of Health 1991, para. 2.4)

Part III and Schedule 2 of the Children Act 1989 marked a radical change from earlier legislation in the degree of importance accorded family support within the overall legislative framework for child care; *and* in the scope and role of family support itself. As Rose suggested, 'The Children Act places a duty on local authorities to safeguard and promote the welfare of children in their area who are in need, and subject to that duty, to promote the upbringing of such children by their families' (Rose 1992, p.ix).

Section 17 (10) of the Act defined a child as being 'in need' if:

> (a) he is unlikely to achieve or maintain, or to have the opportunity of achieving or maintaining, a reasonable standard of health or development without the provision for him of services by the local authority.

> (b) his health or development is likely to be significantly impaired, or further impaired, without the provision for him of such services; or

> (c) he is disabled.

Section 11 specifies that 'development' means physical, intellectual, emotional, social or behavioural development, and 'health' means physical or mental health.

The Children Act 1989 proposed a parent-oriented system of child welfare provision, sharing care and responsibilities between statutory agencies and parents. The emphasis in Section 17 was for local authorities to work with the family and child in the family home (Rose 1992). With respect to provision for children living with their families, the Act (Section 17, subsection 7) outlined the duty of local authorities to make appropriate provision for children in need within their area while they are living with their families. In this sense, services were deemed to include:

- advice, guidance, counselling
- occupational, social, cultural or recreational activities
- home help (which may include laundry facilities)

- facilities for, or assistance with, travelling to and from home for the purpose of taking advantage of any other service provided under this Act or of any similar service

- assistance to enable the child concerned and his family to have a holiday.

The Act specifically included local authorities' duty to respond to children in need by providing family centres (Schedule 2, para. 9) or to facilitate service provision via other organizations, including voluntary and private organizations (Section 17, subsection 5). 'Family centre' was defined as a centre at which any child, parent, carer or person with parental responsibility (subpara. 3) may attend for occupational, social, cultural or recreational activities; for advice, guidance or counselling; or be provided with accommodation while he is receiving advice, guidance or counselling.

In addition, the Act provided a framework for planning family support services:

> Local authorities are required to ensure that a range of services is available to meet the extent of need identified within their administrative areas, including day care provision, for pre-school and school age children, and services to support and improve the strengths and skills of parents in their own homes. Among services to be offered are specified family centres. (Children Act 1989, Schedule 2, para. 9)

It was also made clear that, in designing appropriate policies, local authorities should not restrict support services to families who are already in severe difficulties that pose a risk to children, or to children on the verge of being looked after, or who were returning home from accommodation (Gibbons 1992; Aldgate and Bradley 1999). The requirement for a breadth of planning in respect of children in need is extended by the guidance on children's service planning (Department of Health and Department for Education and Employment 1996), which stresses the need for an integrated approach and a continuum of services available to children and families at different times according to their current needs.

Nevertheless, subsequent to implementation, real progress towards a more equitable balance between those resources allocated to family support and child protection continued to be somewhat tentative with a broadly consistent and rather worrying picture developing of a bias towards child protection as the 1993 report to parliament on the working of the Children Act outlined:

> In general, progress towards full implementation of Section 17 of the Children Act has been slow, and further work is still needed to provide a range of family services aimed at preventing families reaching the point of breakdown. It would appear that some authorities are finding the move from a

reactive social policing role to a more proactive partnership role with families challenging. (Department of Health 1993, para. 2.39)

This common theme across several studies (Giller 1993; Aldgate and Tunstill 1995; Colton *et al.* 1995) was taken up by the Audit Commission, who made a set of specific suggestions to improve the situation. These included a central role for family centres. Such developments, the Commission argued, might also help to de-stigmatize social services support but, at the same time, would not exclude access to a social worker if this were requested or needed (Audit Commission 1994).

In order to acknowledge the broad developmental issues of children in need, the Children Act 1989 had made it explicit that there should be multi-agency working to meet the needs of those eligible for services under Section 17. The introduction of children's service plans made inter-agency working compulsory between social services and other agencies in the planning and provision of services for children in need. Under Section 27 of the Children Act 1989, responsibility lies not only with the social services to support children in need, but also with other local authority and public sector departments such as education, housing, health services and voluntary agencies. In 1995, the Social Services Inspectorate outlined key concepts, such as partnership and inter-agency working. Partnership included:

- intra-local authority departmental co-operation and collaboration

- co-operation and collaboration between local authority social services departments and other public sector organizations (in practice, within social services departments themselves there is a need for joint working, too)

- co-operation and collaboration between local authority social services' departments and voluntary organizations.

Inter-agency working included the following definitions and actions:

- communication: one agency tells another what it intends to do

- consultation: one agency asks another for opinion, information or advice before finalizing plan

- collaboration: independent service provision with joint planning and agreement on responsibilities and boundaries

- bilateral planning: an overlap in service provision with operational interaction arising out of common planning

- joint planning: different agencies working operationally to the same plan.

(See Department of Health, Social Services Inspectorate 1995)

In spite of the recognition of what might promote inter-agency collaboration, gaps remained between policy and practice. Issues related to joint working in practice had been identified earlier in 1991, and included:

- co-ordination as an end rather than a means to an end

- co-ordination to reduce gaps and discontinuities in services resulting in an holistic approach

- (pseudo) solution to problems which lie elsewhere such as ambiguous legislation; confused aims; organisation inertia; professional resistance; inadequate resources.

(Hardiker *et al.* 1991, p.350)

Further, in 1993, attempts had been made to describe impediments to collaboration. Robbins (1993), for example, identified the following barriers:

- structural: fragmentation of service responsibilities across agency boundaries within and between sectors; inter-organisational complexity and lack of clarity of boundaries

- procedural: differences in procedures, planning horizons and cycles

- financial: differences in funding mechanisms and bases; and in stocks and flows of financial resources

- professional: differences in ideologies and values; professional self-interest and concern for threats to autonomy and domain; threats to job security; conflict of views about clients' interests and roles

- status and legitimacy: organisational self interest and concern for threats to autonomy and domain; differences in legitimacy between appointed and elected agencies.

(Robbins 1993, p.89)

A subsequent study by Tunstill and Aldgate, in the series evaluating the Children Act 1989 (see Department of Health 2001) found that many families had multiple needs, which required multi-agency intervention and support prior to, and independently of, any approaches or referrals to social services. However, whilst almost half of the families in the study were referred on to other agencies, few social workers perceived themselves as being referral agents (Tunstill and Aldgate 2000).

Changing policy developments between 1997 and 2003 which have had a major impact on family centres

The New Labour government came into power in 1997 committed to tackling child poverty and social exclusion and to greatly expanding the provision of early years services as part of this. This new spirit was encapsulated in government's aspirations for children as laid out in *Opportunity for All* (HM Treasury 1999):

> Our objective is to create a society in the next two decades in which no child lives in poverty and where all children have opportunities to realise their potential. Improving opportunities for disadvantaged children is at the heart of our strategy. (HM Treasury 1999, p.39)

There were three implicit strands in this set of policies, all of which were likely to have an impact on the work of family centres. The first concerned government's attempts to reduce social deprivation through universal services, such as health and education. A second strand was concerned with income, including the reform of the tax system and increases in some child-related, selective benefits. This strand was also concerned with creating employment opportunities for parents, including lone parents. (These objectives are reflected in subsequent developments such as the National Child Care Strategy (HM Treasury 2004)). The third policy strand related to the most private areas of family life, and was manifested in a high-profile debate about parenting. A National Family and Parenting Institute had already been established in the 1990s to symbolize the importance of parenting. Increasingly, new interventions were coming on stream which straddled the boundary between 'child welfare' and the justice system, including the introduction, by the Criminal Justice Act 2003, of Parenting Orders for those parents who were seen as being unable to control their children. A heightened government focus on adoption of looked-after children emerged, with targets for numbers of children to be adopted set for local authorities by the Department of Health's Quality Protects Initiative (Department of Health 1998; Thoburn 2002). Such a strategy has been questioned by some commentators on the grounds that it overwhelmed and overshadowed efforts to provide family support for birth families (Tunstill 2002).

In a relatively short period of time, the parameters of the debate around children and families' services had changed. In other words, the government's view was that most parents would be able to have their needs met within the newly enhanced universal services, such as health and education. The implication for parents for whom this was not a sufficient answer was that they needed a more hands-on approach, increasingly referred to by central government as 'targeted intervention'. Such intervention might sometimes need 'robust enforcement' (see Hendrick 2003).

Some of the challenges for the task of parenting had been explored in the cross-cutting Comprehensive Spending Review of children and families' services undertaken by the Treasury in 1998 (HM Treasury 1998). Spending reviews tend to set firm and fixed departmental expenditure limits and define the key improvements that the public can expect from these resources. The 1998 cross-cutting review looked at services for young children from a starting point of increasing government concern that current provision of services appeared in many cases to be failing those in greatest need. One of its major concerns was the inadequacy of existing mainstream service responses and the central outcome of the review was the Sure Start Programme (see Glass 1999).

Sure Start local programmes formed a key building block in government's efforts to tackle child poverty and social exclusion (Tunstill *et al.* 2005). New Labour policy in respect of children and families' services has consistently highlighted the value of area-based provision. Sure Start represented an example of new approaches to children and families that were not located in any one mainstream agency. Since 1997, as well as Sure Start, a range of community-based initiatives has been introduced, including Connexions and On Track.

The fact that, from 1997 onwards, policies in respect of children and families were dominated by area-based initiatives has had several organizational and workforce consequences for both mainstream and voluntary agencies. Several of these, as the study will show, had a direct impact on family centres. Overwhelmingly, the construction of new, area-level partnerships has also brought with it an increase in the complexity of funding for many agencies, including the need for repeated, competitive bidding. There has been an increasing diversity of funding at a local level, and in the period under study, funding streams for mainstream agencies such as social services were complemented by funding to the new partnership boards involving complex and contested bidding processes from a range of providers.

As we will explain in subsequent chapters, family centres found themselves at the centre of this major shift in policy for services to support children and families. Whereas the Children Act 1989 had placed family centres at the heart of family support services in the community, the new policy developments produced challenges to their core position. These policy changes introduced a range of area-based agencies, which might, at any one time, be both supporters of and rivals to family centres. For example, because the incomers shared the commitment of the family centre to supporting young children and their families, a Sure Start local programme might provide funding for a local family centre. On the other hand, were the geographical boundaries of the local programme to exclude a local family centre, then that family centre's existing financial instability could be further undermined. If family centres were beginning to struggle, further change was afoot, which would compound these existing challenges.

The policy implications of *Every Child Matters* and the Children Act 2004

If the above developments reflect the intensity of government's interest in children's and family services between 1997 and 2003, the rate of statutory, professional, and organizational change in the child welfare world has increased sharply after 2003. New requirements introduced since 2003 are in the process of reshaping both the structure and, indeed, the political economy of services at the local level. As has so often been the case in child welfare history, major changes in policy and practice have followed the death of a child. In 2003, the Laming Inquiry into the death of Victoria Climbié (CM 5730, 2003), painted a picture of dangerous fragmentation between the key agencies at local level, such as health, education, police and social services. Government responded by setting in train a widespread programme of organizational reform in children's services, and a set of plans to improve outcomes for all children and young people, including the most disadvantaged, in the Green Paper, *Every Child Matters* (CM 5860, 2003). In this paper, five outcomes for children are specified:

- being healthy
- staying safe
- enjoying and achieving
- making a positive contribution
- achieving economic well-being.

In order for these five outcomes to be realized, radical changes are being introduced in the whole system of children's services. These include:

- the improvement and integration of universal services – in early years settings, schools and the health service
- more specialized help to promote opportunity, prevent problems and act early and effectively if and when problems arise
- the reconfiguration of services around the child and family in one place, e.g. children's centres, extended schools and the bringing together of professionals in multi-disciplinary teams
- dedicated and enterprising leadership at all levels of the system
- the development of a shared sense of responsibility across agencies for safeguarding children and protecting them from harm
- listening to children, young people and their families when assessing and planning service provision, as well as in face-to-face delivery.

(Department for Education and Skills 2004a, p.4)

The main proposals of *Every Child Matters* have been incorporated in the Children Act 2004, whose clauses seek to achieve reforms in four key areas: early intervention; accountability and co-ordination; supporting parents and carers; and the introduction of a cross-sector workforce strategy. The Children

Bill received royal assent on 15 November 2004, and seeks to provide a 'legislative spine' for the wider strategy for improving children's lives. It covers the universal services which every child accesses, and more targeted services for those with additional needs. Its declared, overall intention is to improve the quality of working in single disciplines and agencies and increase the extent and quality of multi-disciplinary working. It aims to do this by encouraging integrated planning, commissioning, co-ordination and, where appropriate, delivery of services. As the wording of the Children Act 2004 makes clear, the legislation is intended to be enabling rather than prescriptive, and provides local authorities with some degree of flexibility in the way they implement its provisions.

At the very highest level of the children's services system, *Every Child Matters* has required the transfer of national responsibility for children's services from the Department of Health to the Department for Education and Skills. At the local level, it has required the introduction of a new post of Director of Children's Services to take on responsibility for all local authority social care services for children and all the responsibilities presently held by the local authority acting as Local Education Authority. Additionally, the Director of Children's Services holds the lead role in ensuring that strategic arrangements are in place for the co-ordinated commissioning of health, education, social care and voluntary sector to provide universal and targeted services. The Director also has the lead role in the setting up and monitoring of the replacements for the Area Child Protection Committees, called Local Children's Safeguarding Boards, which are put on a stronger legal footing than their predecessors. The local authority social services departments (with their traditional responsibility for both adult and children's services) have now ceased to exist. Strategic planning and responsibility for delivery or commissioning of a range of social care services for adults will remain within local authority and be headed by a Director of Adult Social Care Services.

Alongside the benefits of clearer responsibility for children's services and the potential for greater integration comes the risk of a less coherent service, for example, for young carers and for the assessment and provision of services to adults with disabilities who are also parents whose children are 'in need'. Although the term 'children's trust arrangements' is frequently used in government policy documents and circulars, the Children Act 2004 does not create 'children's trusts' as statutory organizations, but encourages and facilitates the development of collaborative working and strategic planning. There is some overlap between 'local children's strategic boards' and 'children's trusts' with, sometimes, both of these bodies co-existing and, in other areas, 'children's trust arrangements' being subsumed as part of children's strategy boards. The use of the term 'children's trust', at least in the early stages, led to some confusion, as the term 'trust' has come to be understood as a legal entity with responsibility for provision of a service, for example, a hospital trust, whereas 'children's trust arrangements' or 'children's strategy boards' are top level arrangements, voluntarily entered into by all the key statutory and independent sector agencies who provide services to children within a local authority area to jointly plan and commission services.

These new arrangements will not necessitate structural change or staff transfers; if localities want to transfer staff or create new accountability structures this is a matter for local discretion. Through these over-arching bodies, it is anticipated that there will be increased pooling of budgets and resources across what were traditionally education services (including schools), children's social services, Connexions, certain health services and, in some areas, youth offending teams (YOTs), and the criminal justice services. They may involve, in a non-executive capacity, other organizations that do not pool their budgets, and thereby involve other stakeholders, including the voluntary sector. It is expected that the voluntary and community sectors and parents, young people and community members will be involved in strategic planning through membership of these bodies and will help to make decisions about priorities and the future direction of services. Agencies will continue to fulfil their statutory functions either directly or through commissioning from the voluntary or independent sectors, but it is anticipated that, as the children's trust arrangements become embedded in their local areas, more services will be provided on an inter-agency basis.

While the national roll-out of trusts is still in the comparatively early stages, some messages are already emerging from Phase 1 of a national evaluation of the 35 pilot areas (University of East Anglia and National Children's Bureau 2005). Work by Bachmann *et al.* (in press) describes the early implementation of the 'pathfinders' trusts although, as the authors point out, because the 'pathfinders' were selected even before *Every Child Matters* was published, some bear more resemblance to the proposed model of children's trust arrangements than others. All of these 'pathfinders' had established a children's trust board or equivalent structure, on which health, education and social services were represented along with other agencies including youth offending teams, the voluntary sector, as well as parents and carers. Fifteen of these pathfinders reported widespread joint commissioning of multiple services across two or three of the health, education and social services sectors. The majority also reported bringing together front-line professionals from across the health, education and social services sectors.

The Phase 1 report of the national evaluation of children's trusts (University of East Anglia and National Children's Bureau 2005) also identified a set of factors which facilitated integration of service delivery and improved collaboration between professional groups, including joint training of staff, maintenance of a stable workforce, and a commitment to integration which manifested itself in operational activities such as regular joint meetings, creating a representative structure for planning, and setting up inter-agency working groups to address specific challenges. There was evidence that pre-existing inter-agency relationships proved helpful in establishing the new trusts, and respondents stressed the positive benefits of importance of working in an incremental style and at a slow pace.

There were some barriers to implementation. The perceived general barriers identified in the evaluation included: complex geographical service interfaces; inadequate resources for the development of new services when the mainstream services are already over-stretched in many areas; ring-fenced budgets; lack of time; the existence of multiple initiatives and multiple targets; changes in management; and difficulties around the recruitment and retention of staff. There were additional specific barriers to engaging with the voluntary sector. These included: short-term funding; high staff turnover in voluntary agencies; absence of a co-ordinating mechanism; and tensions between the voluntary and statutory sectors around the concept and practice of 'targeting'.

Related changes of relevance to family centres include the replacement of the earlier government requirement to plan, consult and publish 'children's services plans' (Department of Health and Department for Education and Employment 1996), by the requirement in the Children Act 2004 for councils and their partner agencies to produce 'children and young people's plans'. This is a central early task for children's strategy boards and children's trust arrangements. Amongst other aspects of the plans, it is anticipated that they will encourage the development of appropriate numbers of children's centres, appropriately cited, which will work closely with extended schools and the mainstream health and children's social care services. It is intended that mainstream services work from a range of co-located and multi-disciplinary teams, and there will also be arrangements for 'out-posting' and 'attaching' of health, social care and other staff to the children's centres and extended schools. There is some uncertainty as to the extent to which, in reality, such services will be seamless. For example, schools and teachers, and stakeholders in primary care trusts, such as GPs, are not legally required to co-operate. Parallels have already been drawn with the coincidental implementation of the Children Act 1989 and the NHS and Community Care Act 1991(Hudson 2005). In this earlier period, because of competing philosophies and resources, tensions and gaps appeared in what was intended by the Children Act 1989 to be a holistic and co-ordinated response to both need and risk in families (Tunstill *et al.* 1995).

In parallel with the setting up of the new children's services directorates and children's trust arrangements, it is also intended that a new nationwide database will now keep track of every one of the eleven million children in England. There will be a unique identifier for each child, which will be used on the records of all statutory agencies and basic details on the child such as date of birth and names of those with parental responsibility. Discussions are continuing, in 2006, about what information and which agencies will routinely be included and about data protection safeguards, accuracy checks and costs.

Linked to this, national guidance is being developed and local systems devised and piloted on arrangements for a Common Assessment Framework (CAF) (Department for Education and Skills 2004b). This system will set in place common assessment processes and the sharing of file information between agencies, when it becomes clear that the more complex needs of a child and/or parents require a co-ordinated multi-agency approach and additional services not available from any one agency. Having triggered an assessment process and, as appropriate, meetings between professionals and parents, a 'lead professional' will be identified who, with the family members, will co-ordinate the services provided and help family members to identify needs and insist that they are met. Common Assessment Frameworks and Lead Professional arrangements in twelve pilots are currently being evaluated with a view to issuing further guidance in 2006 (see Department for Education and Skills website 2006: www.dfes.gov.uk). The Local Safeguarding Boards will continue to focus on services for children who are suffering or at risk of being maltreated, as well as having a wider remit to ensure that preventive services are in place to minimize maltreatment and impairment to development.

In addition to this emphasis on the creation of comprehensive service networks to meet a range of levels and types of need, *Every Child Matters* and the subsequent Children Act 2004 are also distinctive in acknowledging the crucial role of the workforce, both in relation to composition, quantity and quality, and in optimizing or minimizing the chances of achieving the five outcomes in *Every Child Matters*. A Children's Workforce Development Unit has been established to help enhance the role of the workforce through training, career development, and improved staff mobility, as well as encouraging better integration (Department for Education and Skills 2005). It represents workers across the statutory and independent sectors, including early years, education welfare, learning mentors, Connexions, foster care and social care.

Directors of children's services and lead members will be required to lead the creation of integrated workforce strategies that respond to local need, including induction training for all recruits to the common core of skills; and knowledge and training for development to support the introduction of a lead professional role. The Unit is, through its published strategy, working towards a single qualifications framework for the children's workforce; and plans to have in place an early years professional in all of the 3500 planned children's centres by 2010; and in every day care setting by 2015 (Department for Education and Skills 2005).

However, two components of the changes stand out as absolutely crucial to current and future family centre activity. These are the phased introduction over an eight-year period, from 2002, of 3500 children's centres and the introduction of 'extended schools'. Between these two new 'institutions', one dealing with pre-school, the latter with school-age children, government intends that local communities will have widely enhanced and non-stigmatizing access to child and family services. Below is highlighted the significance to family centres of current requirements for children's centres (which are, at the time of writing, rather more advanced than the plans for extended schools).

The children's centres concept was developed in the run-up to the 2002 spending review settlement and promoted in the inter-departmental child care review published in November 2002, entitled Developing Integrated Services for Young Children and their Families (Performance and Innovation Unit, HM Government 2002). The review concluded that the weight of evidence supported a rationale for investment in good quality integrated child care for disadvantaged pre-school children.

The 2002 Spending Review by the Treasury provided funds to support the establishment of children's centres for pre-school children in the 20 per cent most disadvantaged wards in England. As part of the government's commitment to reducing funding streams, the funding for children's centres has been brought together with some of the money for new 'neighbourhood nursery' places into a single resource of £435m. A target has been established to reach 650,000 pre-school children with children's centre services by March 2006 ('reach' meaning the number of children potentially able to access services – i.e. those in a children's centre catchment area). There is also a target for 2500 children's centres by 2008 and 3500 by 2010 (HM Treasury 2004). Local authorities have been given targets for reaching children with children's centre services and creating new full day care places and, by January 2004, 67 settings had been 'early designated' as children's centres, in other words, models for the way the network would develop around the country.

Guidance on children's centres, published by the Department for Education and Skills in December 2005, which took account of various evaluations commissioned by government, including the National Evaluation of Sure Start, highlights several issues of consequence for family centres:

- Local authorities should make better use of information and tailor services more directly to the needs and interests of families.

- There should be a greater emphasis on outreach and home visiting, especially with families which would be unlikely to visit a children's centre.

- Children's centres should offer services that are attractive to parents but not lose sight of their primary purpose – to improve children's life chances.

- There should be better integrated and joined-up working, allowing information to be shared about where families live.

- There should be families' improved personalization of the delivery of services, so they are provided in ways which meet individual needs and encourage them to take up services.

The guidance makes clear that local authorities should offer specific services in a specific way. This is known as the 'core offer'. The following excerpt from the children's centre guidance conveys a sense of the new requirements:

> Parents and families should have access to the support they need irrespective of where they live. This is why below, for the first time, we set out clearly the services that should be made available to all families with children under five. These are not new services, but setting them out in this way provides Local Authorities with a clear framework in which to work.
>
> In order to ensure the best possible outcomes for every child, we believe that parents and families with children under five should expect one of three broad levels of service, according to their need.

(Department for Education and Skills December 2005, p.9)

Local authority or NHS services should offer all families with children under five:

- Free early years provision (integrated early education and care) for 12.5 hours a week, 33 weeks a year for three and four year olds. This free early years provision will increase to 38 weeks a year from 2006 and to 15 hours a week by 2010.

- Information and access to child care in the local area.

- Information on parenting, drop in groups and opportunities to access parenting support and education.

- Ante-natal and post-natal services, child health services and information on health.

- Information about employment, education and training.

- Information at points of transition, including information sessions around the time of the birth of their child (by linking to and building on existing ante-natal and post-natal services) and on entry to primary school which, as part of the extended schools programme, will be offering sessions for parents as their child starts school.

(Department for Education and Skills December 2005, p.10)

The scale and scope of these aspirations for organizational and strategic change are clearly extensive. Many aspects of these policy directions, of which the above represent only the most obvious examples, pose considerable implications for the future work of family centres, and vice versa. We can certainly identify five key themes in the policy changes required by *Every Child Matters*, where the experience of family centres, captured in our study's findings, can provide lessons and insights to those engaged in the implementation and delivery process. These lessons include:

- maximizing the range of early intervention services
- involving the statutory and the independent sectors
- working across organizational and professional divides
- recruiting, developing and retaining the children's workforce
- striking the right balance between centre-based and outreach-delivered services.

The study reported in this book coincided with several phases in the evolution of these new policy directions, and captured, from the perspective of family centres, the challenges they now pose for every agency. For example, the traditional and highly regarded activities of family centres have very often spanned the entire continuum of the *safeguarding* and *promoting* of the welfare of the children in the communities where they are located. In addition, their parentage, which includes both statutory and voluntary agencies, has compounded uncertainty in terms of funding and identity. They have had to cope with the advent of new area-based initiatives, including, in some cases, the haemorrhage of staff from pre-existing family support services to the more glamorous and better paid posts in Sure Start.

There is inevitably some irony in a study to explore the networking and co-ordinating functions of family centres being commissioned just at the very time when the tectonic plates of the children and family services system were about to start shifting beneath their feet. Throughout this period, family centres have found themselves at what must have seemed to many of them the eye of the storm. However, their ability to draw on very relevant experience, and their in-depth understanding of the challenges involved, means that family centres can provide and share with partners a range of lessons for the successful accomplishment of the tasks which lie ahead.

In short, we believe the account in the following chapters provides an opportunity for policy makers, in the process of developing children's centres and extended schools, to draw on the long-standing expertise, skills and experience of their local family centres. In doing so, they can only optimize their agencies' success in implementing the new *Every Child Matters* requirements. Even if the terminology has changed, the experience of family centres can provide a solid foundation for the development of new structures and ways of working. We now turn, in the following chapters, to an in-depth exploration of their activities across a range of key areas.

Chapter 3

Building Links and Partnerships with Other Agencies

The new children's agenda highlights the potential impact that good partnerships between agencies can have on the services they both offer and provide to children and their parents in a local area. For example, as the Audit Commission recognized back in 1994 (a recognition which was the original starting point for this study), family centres potentially occupy an important place within a wider network of agencies, both inside and beyond their immediate communities:

> Social Services support is focused too narrowly at present ... an investment in more proactive services should improve the possibility of reducing the need for crisis intervention... the idea of a 'primary resource' or the one stop shop family centre could act as a single point of entry to a range of multi-agency support services. (Audit Commission 1994, p.46)

Two key characteristics distinguish family centres from many other agencies. First, as indicated above, they clearly possess the potential to act as a *one stop shop*. Second, their location within a complex matrix of community stakeholders, including individuals, services and other agencies, places them at the potential heart of any local service configuration. They were, for example, in the 1990s, developing responses to the needs of ethnic minority services users in local areas (Butt and Box 1998). Even the most imaginative day care setting would not have the potential to offer the same wide-ranging package of services as a family centre. In the early 1990s, as Smith (1996) suggests, family centres were beginning to explore:

> the viability of combining different styles of work in one centre. For example, Penn Green Centre in Corby ... combines nursery provision for children with intensive social work support for families, a range of groups and activities, adult education, and schemes run by parents. Fulford in Bristol ... combining

family therapy and community development approaches, set out to consider the relationship between the centre and its neighbourhood. (Smith 1996, p.11)

Then, as now, it is the location of services, be they family centres or children's centres, which can have a major positive or, indeed, negative impact on access to services. The task of facilitating accessibility depends on close liaison and co-operation between a range of community stakeholders, including individuals, services, agencies and projects.

Their potential for maximizing access is a major asset for centres, especially those which are capable of providing a broad range of services, compared with other 'single purpose' family support services. It anticipates some of the current concerns of policy makers. Indeed current government guidance on children's centres suggests they should aim to offer information, advice and support to parents, as well as early years provision (i.e. integrated child care and early learning), health services, family support, parental outreach and employment advice for disadvantaged families (see Department for Education and Skills July 2005).

In this chapter, we explore how family centres have paved the way for planning and delivering some of these new partnerships. Their experiences provide a useful foundation for the development of children's centres within the new children's services agenda.

Understanding links and partnerships with other agencies

First, because working alongside others within a complex network of services is so much a part of the identity of family centres, we wanted to understand how the family centres built up and sustained links with other agencies and how they forged ongoing operational partnerships.

There was a complex range of links with local organizations, both statutory and voluntary. The diverse functions and identities of the agencies presented differing challenges for family centres. Inevitably, the task of relating to other agencies was dominated by connections with social services departments.

Over three quarters of family centres had links with other agencies in and outside their immediate area. In some cases, these links were quite formal, including funding agreements with statutory agencies, such as social services or health. In other cases links developed from informal community connections. Where family centres were active in a range of formal links with statutory agencies, they also tended to have developed a range of informal links in the community, and through families' own support systems. By contrast, where family centres had few links formally with other agencies, they were equally isolated from wider community connections.

The range of links with other agencies

Using data from the national survey, this study looked at the range of involvement of family centres with different types of organizations. This quantitative data was complemented by using data from interviews with family centre managers. The interviews provided the opportunity to look at the processes of linking with different types of organizations.

There was a range of agencies and professionals involved in the provision of family support with which family centres could have links, including social services, GPs, health visitors and other health services, schools and other education services.

The number of links per family centre ranged from none to fifteen but, overall, many family centres had a broad range of links. As Table 3.1 shows, these links sometimes derived from explicit formal policy guidelines applied by the family centre, sometimes from personal relationships and sometimes from both.

Table 3.1 Sources of agency links

Agencies and professionals with which family centres had links	Sources of links and percentage of family centres by source			
	Centre policy	Personal	Both	No links
Social services	55	1	36	8
Health visitors	54	3	35	8
Education services	53	3	32	12
Schools	46	5	30	19
Other health services	41	7	22	30
GPs	36	10	18	36
Other professionals	36	6	15	43

n=415

As can be seen from this table, in over half of the family centres (55%), links with social services derived directly from the policy of the centre itself, as did similar numbers of links with health visitors (54%) and education services (53%). In other words, there was a powerful, explicit commitment on behalf of the centre to constructing policy-driven links, although this did not preclude some links at the personal level. These personal level links were considerably less extensive than those influenced by policy. For example, only 10 per cent of family centres reported personal links with GPs. It may be worth noting that 36 per cent of family centres lacked any links at all with GPs while only 8 per cent lacked any links at all with social services or health visitors.

These figures were reinforced by family centre managers, who gave us examples of the local personnel with whom they were likely to have contact in the course of their networking. Health and education services featured more frequently than social services in family centre managers' descriptions of their network links. Of all the contacts mentioned, a fifth were with health services and around a fifth with education services. During the course of the chapter we will be looking at links with the principal agencies in more detail.

An extract from an interview in a social services' family centre illustrates how some centres had a complex range of links with a wide range of professionals, including teaching staff, health visitors and mental health professionals, involving parents and children:

> We have workers who go into schools and they run small groups with the children who display difficult behaviour in schools. The teachers identify who needs to be part of the group and will talk about what the issues are; what we're trying to do is focus on issues relevant to the age of the children we're working with. These are often round low self esteem, confidence, bullying, protection work – things like that.

> I would try and have a mixed balance in the groups. We may have three children who are quite difficult and then three children who are not experiencing any difficulties in schools. So we get a good role model in amongst this group to help those who are experiencing difficult behaviour.

> We also run parenting programmes with the health visitors – that's a joint venture. They go in and they have a period of time when they provide a drop in session for families. If the parent has a problem that they talk to the teacher about and if the teacher thinks that the centre staff could be of use, then the teacher will ask us to run a group.

> We have what we call 'The Estate Partnership' which again looks at things like anti-truancy and issues on our local estates. So we're part of that. We look at what sort of services are around on the estate and if there's any way we can offer something we do, and we also tell them what's around. Housing, health, schools as well – we've good links with the local GPs.

> A lot of health visiting people work very well with the family centre and if we're due to see a family we haven't seen, we'll ring them up and see if they've already seen them or not. We'll discuss the idea of going to see them together at some stage. So there's an awful lot of dialogue between the family centre and health visitors. There's a lot of different surgeries in our area so it depends really where the family's living as to who we link up.

We also have a child and family unit which has a psychologist attached and does family therapy and we link in with them. We're meeting with them again to look at how we can deliver services between us so that we don't duplicate. I see them as more specialized, so we may do quite a bit of work with a family to a point where it becomes bigger than we can deal with and then we'll refer them on. We have co-worked with families rather than just handing them on if it's been appropriate to do that.

Building links through funding or sponsorship

Our findings showed that an important aspect of making links was the formal links associated with funding. At the same time, it is important to note that managing a centre does not necessarily equate with fully funding it. As Table 3.2 shows, funding derived from a range of sources across England but funding from local authorities was dominant:

- 72 per cent of family centres were part of direct provision by local authorities.

- 68 per cent of family centres were fully funded and 11 per cent were partly funded by local authorities.

Table 3.2 also shows that responsibility for the involvement of other agencies in funding was at a lower level than the funding provided by local authorities. Child care voluntary organizations were minority funders or had non-funding involvement. Health services contributed funding to only four per cent of centres and, of these, funded less than one per cent fully.

Data from the follow-up survey (table not shown) revealed the extent to which local authorities, and particularly social services departments, continued to dominate family centre funding. Seventy-two per cent of our family centres were part of local authority direct provision, 58 per cent of them being an integral part of social services.

Fifty per cent of family centres in the review were fully funded by social services and 8 per cent by other local authority departments, including 4 per cent by education services. Eleven per cent were funded by social services in conjunction with other funders, including, but not restricted to, education services (8%). In addition, 57 per cent of non-local authority family centres had service level agreements with social services.

Sixty-two per cent of family centres in the review survey had a single funder, which was predominantly the local authority. Of the remaining family centres, 44 per cent had more than one funder but were still part of local authority direct provision.

Where family centres were not part of social services direct provision, funding was likely to come from more than one source and be more diverse. A range of tasks and bidding activity was likely to be involved as well as diversity in respect of how long funding might last. These non-local authority part-funders included initiatives such as Sure Start, the Children's Fund and Single Regeneration Budget, health service initiatives, child care voluntary organizations and, finally, lottery money and charities.

Table 3.2 Family centre sponsorship/funding (national survey)

Source	% of family centres		
	Managed by	Fully funded by	Partially funded by
Local authority	72	68	11
Health services	Less than one	Less than one	4
Barnardo's	4	2	22
Children's Society	3		
NCH Action for Children	14		
NSPCC	Less than one		
Other	5	Less than one	3

n=415

Building links through referrals

A further set of links was associated with the individuals or agencies who referred families to the centres. Our national survey data showed that the majority of family centres can be accessed by referral either as the *only* mode of access (34%) or *in combination with* open access to services (55%). Using data from the survey, we looked at the range of referral sources and the involvement of different organizations. To give a rounded picture of the referral processes, we draw on data from interviews with family centre managers.

The range of referral links

The number of referral sources per family centre ranged from none to eleven. There was a range of referral sources, shown in Table 3.3 below. The majority of family centres took referrals from social services. Although health services are minority funders and sponsors, they represent a substantial source of family centre referrals, with around half of family centres having referrals from health visitors and a quarter from other health professionals. There were also just under a quarter of referrals from voluntary agencies. Around a third of the

Table 3.3 Sources of referrals (national survey)

Sources of referrals	% of family centres
Social services	81
Health visitor	48
Informal: self, family etc.	35
Voluntary agencies	24
Other health	23
School	18
GP	8
Community	5
Other	13

n=415

Note: Centres took referrals for several sources simultaneously, so percentages add up to more than 100 per cent.

family centres accepted informal referrals from the community, from family or directly from parents.

These referral patterns may well raise questions about the way in which pooled budgets are discussed, agreed and deployed between different agencies in the context of the new 'children's services authorities'. To put it bluntly, why should the local authority be expected to pay for all of the services, when, in fact, health trusts are making significant use of them at the same time but failing to contribute to the same level?

The profound influence of social services on the work of the family centres was clear from the review data on referrals accepted and services provided in response to referrals. Table 3.4 shows that, at the review survey, 31 per cent of family centres accepted referrals from social services exclusively (compared to 21% in the national survey) and that, overall, referrals were more likely to come from social services than from any other source.

In other words, family centres participating in the review survey provided a higher proportion of their services in response to referrals from social services than they did in response to referrals from other sources. Table 3.5 below shows that when family centres in the review survey received a referral from social services, they were highly likely to take it on and provide all or most of the services requested. This was not necessarily the case with referrals from other sources.

Table 3.4 Referrals (review survey)

Referrals	% of family centres
Referrals only from social services	31
Social services and other sources about the same number of referrals	28
More referrals from social services than from other sources	21
More referrals from other sources than from social services	12
Referrals only from sources other than social services	4
No referrals	4

n=344

Table 3.5 Services for referrers (review survey)

Services provided to referred families	Source of referrals and percentage of family centres providing services	
	Social services	Other sources
All/most services requested	59	25
About half the services requested	15	27
A few services	18	15
No services	8	33

n=344

As well as receiving and/or responding to referrals, family centres can refer on to other sources of family support. Our interview data suggested that this process both facilitates, and is facilitated by, the networks and links which family centres have built up.

For example, staff told us:

> You can ring people up and they'll say 'Just do us a report but consider it read. But I need the report to action it'.

> Suddenly I'm working much better with education than we have ever done. I meet regularly with Special Educational Needs Service, particularly because a lot of our children have been identified as being at Stages One and Two of

special educational needs. All the family centres have somebody who carries out a statementing role so they co-ordinate services for those children – make sure the pre-teaching services get involved. We refer directly now to an educational psychologist. We never used to be able to do that. So we've been able to make sure that we're meeting that child's needs. Before we'd have to go via the health route to get a referral to that service and that could take six to eight months sometimes; that service is changing all the time and they're getting more targeted.

We have a group of professionals … who, fortuitously if you like, are committed to working together. I don't think there's any professional I can think of who works in our area in the child care field who stands on their dignity of saying, 'This is mine. I'm not going to share this with you'. And we can fast track. That's the other good thing. We don't get this nonsense that I've experienced before – if somebody rings me and says, 'I've got a family that I think needs to come to your centre,' I say, 'Fine, OK, give me the details'. If I ring the educational psychologist or CPN [community psychiatric nurse] or whatever and I say, 'I need some advice' or 'I think this is something that needs you,' they say, 'That's fine'. There's none of this, 'Oh well! I need to do my own assessment. I can't just take your word for it'.

Building links through participation in government and other initiatives

Data from the national survey showed that family centres were involved in a range of government and other initiatives. Our interviews with family centre managers explored their involvement in these initiatives.

Types of initiative

Table 3.6 shows the level of actual, planned and non-involvement by family centres, in a range of initiatives, at the time of the national survey.

Quality Protects was, unsurprisingly, given the timing of the study, the initiative with highest participation, with over half the family centres directly involved. This was a programme launched in 1998 with the aim of transforming the management and delivery of children's services for whom local authorities had direct responsibilities (see Quinton 2004). Early years development and child care programmes were a link for over half of the family centres too, although only 18 per cent were involved in Early Excellence programmes. The limited focus of family centres on school-age children might explain the relatively low participation in Out of School New Opportunities and Education Action Zone programmes.

Level of involvement in government and other initiatives

The number of government initiatives in which family centres were involved ranged from none to eleven. Family centres were classified according to their range of involvement as high involvement (above the average, which was three) and low involvement (equal to or below average). Overall, slightly more family centres had a lower rather than higher level of involvement in government and other initiatives.

Table 3.6 Involvement in government initiatives and other initiatives

Initiatives	Percentage of family centres			
	Involved		Not involved	
	Actual	*Planned*	*None*	*Unaware*
Quality Protects	55	12	28	5
Early years development and child care programmes	52	13	33	2
Single regeneration budget programmes	24	11	58	7
Sure Start	22	26	48	4
Early Excellence	18	12	65	5
Out of School New Opportunities	13	13	62	12
Education Action Zone	12	6	70	12
Health Action Zone	11	11	67	11
Healthy Living	10	14	63	13
New Deal for Communities	8	11	67	14
Other	11	2	87	0

n=415

There were regional variations within the overall distribution, with more family centres in the North and Midlands likely to have high-level involvement in initiatives, as compared to the South and London. This was the only significant association between regional location and other key variables.

Naturally, involvement with initiatives was not limited to local authority social services' family centres, with interview data showing that small independent family centres could also be in the frame:

> We've accessed this European funding. All right, it was in partnership with social services but we played a big part in that they wouldn't have got it without us. Social services are the lead agency in that they put together the business plan – they've got the expertise to do that – but we were consulted every step of the way and we made sure we were. We're not your fly-by-night, run by a couple of ladies who meet once a month in the front room or in the pub or whatever! We're very well organized.

Participation in initiatives in turn reflected further opportunities for the development of family centres, and for enlarging their support networks:

> We became part of various scenarios and panels – the Refocusing Group, all kinds of panels – the domestic violence forum, the this forum, the that forum, the other forum – you get to be on all of them! We get to work with agencies like the Alcohol and Drug Advisory Service, mental health teams and various others. So the will to work in that way has been present here for as long as I can remember. I think that's a tribute to the various teams and practitioners that right from the beginning they welcomed our approach and climbed aboard and wanted to use the system. So there is already that networking in place. And obviously, that's on a fieldwork level. We then, in the fullness of time, began to be involved in what you might call the next tier of management for consultancy purposes. For example, if they were consulting for a children's services plan or whatever, we were contributing to shaping it. Then we became involved in the Early Years Partnership which extended that quite wide remit.

Family centres with key roles in programmes such as Sure Start could contribute to implementation of this government initiative, by exploiting their existing links:

> So that when Sure Start came along – we were also involved in the Excellence Initiative which again was taking us another tier up the organizational ladders and the agencies that are actually on the Sure Start partnership are health, social services, education, Learning Support, National Childminders Association, Pre-School Learning Association. And it has representation from various community groups.

At the same time, participation in the Sure Start programme could develop and strengthen those links:

> It hasn't changed all that much. The network was already there and pretty good. I probably communicate significantly further up the ladder now – at times – but routinely, on a day-to-day basis, it's the same level practitioners.

Indeed, even tenuous involvement in high-profile initiatives such as Sure Start could facilitate and augment contact with other sources of support:

> The local health visitors, GPs are involved in the steering group for Sure Start. And certainly in the last six months, while I've been involved in that, I think I've got to know more people in the area than I previously knew from going to smaller groups. I spend a lot of time and some of those meetings and groups are really useful and others are not so useful. Clearly, the Sure Start one is.

These networks could be productive, in terms of collecting information about the identity and availability of local support:

> Even though we're not going to be a Sure Start programme as such, we'll be involved in providing services within that Sure Start programme and just attending those meetings has opened everybody's understanding of the work that everyone else is doing. Again, people know each other better. People are clearer about who's doing what. And from that, I would expect that people are clearer about who to go to for various things. It's an issue of signposting – Sure Start is obviously really key. People know where to access provision and are able to send people to the right place.

Benefits were anticipated from family centre workers transferring all or part of their time to Sure Start and other programmes:

> After April, a lot of Sure Start services will run from here as well because there isn't a building at the moment. And we'll be part of that as well. There'll be a transitional phase and I'm anticipating that our key workers will do joint work with Sure Start. Some of the groups we run at the moment like Young Parents, Time Out have a family centre worker who is responsible for them. That worker will stay within the family centre but I don't anticipate that he will give up his role in Time Out.* I think that will continue. There will be lots of cross working and link working.

> * (Structured drop in centre)

Ongoing partnership work with other agencies

Although social services clearly dominated the day-to-day work and, sometimes, the overall operation of family centres, the majority of family centres in the study had similar levels of involvement with health and education services.

Partnership work with health services

Health professionals were found to work frequently in partnership with family centre workers. Although health services were unlikely to be major funders of family centre work, they could be a substantial source of referrals; and have links with family centres in relation to service development and delivery. For example, there was evidence that health service and family centre staff could be working very closely together:

> In fact, quite often we, in the family centre, feel like we've got more in common with those in health than we have with social services. They won't fund us, no. I mean the nearest we've got to applying for funding from them – we ran a group with a health visitor and a CPN for women who are post-natally depressed – and that happened by accident – but it's quite useful. It's a really good service but it's clearly preventative. We jointly work – it's a group that meets every week and one of my workers runs it with a CPN or a health visitor. And the referrals generally come from health although they might come via social services. In fact, referrals come mostly from GPs and health visitors.

Links with health visitors were often particularly strong. Sharing clients, interests and pressures meant that the two services were often working closely together:

> The links are good. And that's because we've worked really hard. And they're round the corner. We've done joint work on handling children's behaviour. They come to Allocation. I'm chair of the poverty action group and health visitors come to that but that's because they feel part of what's happening in the area. It is also because of the networks we've built. If there's nobody to sustain them, if there's nobody to make those links, they can wither. I ring them up and say, 'We've got a meeting about so and so', and she'll come round. If those links will go, I don't know what we will do. It's hard work making them. Links take time to make and they need to be worked on and nurtured. If there's nobody to do that or nobody thinks it's important, we're back to square one where health visitors don't get anything from social services.

We found that family centres often positively initiated links with various aspects of the health service, in relation to both formal collaborative work through their respective organizations and less formal discussion of issues:

> We've got some excellent links in fact with the mental health teams. We've got very good links with GP surgeries and health visitors. We've got school nursing links. We've got paediatricians in the local hospital so we've got a very good linking protocol. We try to have regular meetings. We've just had a lunch with the community mental health team. So the two teams met and talked about similar issues like the new assessment framework and what the implications would be for the joint protocols. So those protocols are useful as a starting point and mean that lots of families with children come here and use post-natal depression group. We've got the mental health group which is actually for women who've got mental health problems who are parents or mothers who meet here. They're run jointly by the community mental health teams and by ourselves. We do have input from other agencies as well. So

anything I'm telling you is pretty substantial and mostly covered by some form of protocol.

Links with individual health personnel

The main links with individual health service personnel were with health visitors. Family centre managers explained that GPs were more likely to be 'outsiders', and only linked indirectly to family centre work:

> We don't link directly with the doctors. We tend to work more through the health visitors and more through their nursery officer. But the health visitors know us. The GPs know us. So that's the filtering, they will go through that route.

> When I was a field worker, if I had my child protection hat on, it was different then because there was a lot of contact with GPs and it was often through Section 47 investigations. Nowadays, of course, it could also be through looked-after children in terms of the requirements around medicals. The family centre itself now has very little contact with GPs other than if we make contact ourselves.

Generally health visitors served to mediate between GPs and family centres. One manager told us that their link with health was primarily with health visitors and, to a lesser extent, with the child and adolescent mental health service. She explained that GPs were likely to become involved only in child protection or late intervention work and, even then, not necessarily directly:

> A GP would say to a health visitor, 'I'm concerned about this family. Would you put a referral in to the family centre?' And the same applies in child protection reviews. The GP is very rarely there. He would expect the health visitor to give his account of the work.

Ongoing partnership work with schools and education services

Here, partnership working underpinned services for children and their parents, whether as individual children, individual parents or as groups of people dealing with similar challenging issues, such as domestic violence. In some cases, the partnerships could be harnessed in a very purposive way to deal with particular child and family circumstances. Such work is particularly important in relation to child development issues, such as children making the transition from nursery to school. It might include ensuring that information about any special needs and problems is appropriately shared:

> There are several schools we work with locally where children from this centre go. So obviously, letters and phone calls explaining the child's needs are helpful as is going to their allocation meetings. A member of staff will go to those. Members of staff from the nursery visit us, joining the family support

groups to talk to the parents about local nurseries. They also get to meet the staff there. Obviously, if the child's name is on the child protection register, education staff attend the monitoring meetings. If there are problems with children during school then the family support worker will go to the school or have meetings here with mum and the teacher.

Proximity clearly helped to facilitate such ongoing partnerships. We visited a family centre where the fact that it was next door to the school was seen as a positive virtue. It meant that the family centre could undertake work with children after the school day.

Links with schools were sometimes restricted to negotiating time off school for children to participate in work with parents:

> So we do quite a bit of work from that school. Other children that have gone to nursery school but the parents still need to be here, so the schools will release them for one day to come here so we can carry on bits of work that we've been doing. We do liaise very carefully with everybody and they liaise with us, which is nice.

There was also evidence of close liaison for specific projects to prevent family breakdown. Several managers explained that they had developed the practice of meeting regularly with head teachers in local secondary schools. This liaison enabled them to support the child's regular attendance at school and to ensure that they were aware of the needs of the children in the school holidays. In most cases, they made sure that the more challenging pupils were offered a package of activities and groups which would prevent them from getting into trouble in the school holidays.

In contrast, this high level of liaison tended not to be reflected in comments about the education welfare services. In these cases, partnership was restricted to referrals based on little and, sometimes, inadequate information:

> We try to work in conjunction with the education welfare service, although I do sometimes wonder what the hell they do really. Because when they get a problem – they might just as well put their 'phones on divert to us. But we do try to work with them and, after all, it is better they refer to us than not.

Links with agencies focused on children and young people

There was evidence of a range of links with agencies focusing on children and young people, including local authority services such as: child and adolescent family services; child and family services; child guidance clinics; nurseries; foster carers; youth and community services.

In addition, there were links with voluntary sector children's organizations, such as Barnardo's, National Children's Home (NCH), Children's Society and the NSPCC. We also found links with the key agencies involved in the child protection system, such as area child protection committees, court welfare officers and children's guardians.

Links with specific support agencies

There were links with agencies that had specific support functions such as disability agencies. These included play for children with disabilities, Portage services (a home visiting educational service for pre-school children with additional support or special needs), special need services, speech and language therapists and the Royal National Institute for the Blind. In addition, there were links with agencies meeting the needs of specific minority ethnic groups such as refugee organizations and the Association of African Caribbean Friends. Lastly, there was a group of organizations dealing with specific circumstances ranging from Alcoholics Anonymous to the Army Welfare Service.

Family centres' links with specialist support services such as Refugee Action may complement their own work with families. While families with refugee status could attend family centres for similar reasons to those of other families not associated with their refugee status, there could still be benefits from liaison with specialist support services:

> We have a refugee team actually so we don't have quite so much involvement with them but once your immigration status is confirmed, you're no longer a refugee, of course, and then if there's any tasks or issues there that have been picked up – they are recommended for a place and come to our notice for the same sort of reason that other people would. But obviously, the families may have particular needs. In these cases, the refugee team are good sources of advice for us so we can offer culturally appropriate support to that family.

A similarly wide range of links was found in relation to agencies providing practical support. This included family aides; furniture projects; domestic violence units; family/child and family therapeutic services; Relate; local and national charities; Citizens' Advice Bureau; leisure services; solicitors; volunteer bureau; Homestart and Welcare.

Links with organizations such as Homestart and Welcare were found to be especially useful to social services' family centres, because of their 'added value' and non-statutory status. Homestart, for example, could supplement practical and emotional family support work; Welcare could offer an acceptable alternative to family centre provision in terms of parenting skills development and personal development opportunities for parents:

> We try to provide family support from a range of different sources where it's viable. We might use Homestart for parents with a number of young children. It's non-stigmatizing again. People feel like they've got someone coming into their homes to help, not there just to check up on them. They're there to do practical tasks and befriend. They do a very good job like that. In turn, I've done some training with Homestart volunteers. Welcare are different because

they have their own packages. They run parenting groups which are very similar to those in the family centre here. They do their own parenting, arts and crafts – they have computers, adult literacy, this sort of thing. In fact, they do a number of things.

The thing about this borough is it depends where you are. We're in one part of the borough whereas Welcare is based right in the other part so hopefully, the patch that we cover between us offers something that most people can reach. It's not all centred around just one place. I think some people might prefer Welcare because again it is non-statutory. Welcare are very good and if there are concerns, they are up front with families and we'll get referrals. Likewise, if we feel that we've worked with a family and a lower level of involvement is still required, Welcare can provide that support so hopefully, there is a sort of balance – we balance each other.

Links with other housing agencies

In their links with housing agencies such as housing departments and associations, hostels for homeless people and women's refuges, family centres may adopt a mediating role between families and 'authority'. Formal liaison by the centre could operate to protect vulnerable families from the worst outcomes, such as eviction:

> We've got a housing adviser that comes in and is currently working with one of our families who has an eviction hanging over their heads. At a meeting yesterday with one of their legal advisers, he said that decisions about kicking people out have got to be bigger than 'good tenant/bad tenant'. This reflects the fact we have a protocol with them now so before they get into any proceedings, they come to us for our assessment of the family. If we say, 'They are improving. You mustn't take action because your responsibilities, under the Children Act Section 18, are greater than just housing.' And that's working quite well. So we're trying to nurture that a little just at the moment.

Links with crime and youth justice agencies

There was evidence of various links with agencies concerned with crime and youth justice, such as the police, the probation service, and youth offending teams:

> We have both statutory and informal links. Obviously, we have our child protection links and that kind of process and joint working. And then there's quite an informal process which is about sharing information and that's intelligence sort of work, which is quite important really. Domestic violence is a huge thing at the moment, as is harassment – those sorts of things. We are making strong links with the new community safety teams, who deliver community support as well. We do a lot of joint work with them, including joint visits.

What the community bobby also does which is absolutely great is if he's around and, if we've got a difficult interview to do, then he'd make his presence felt and on the whole that's worked extremely well. We have never had to make a 999 call from the centre and we have had some very difficult people here.

Links with various other agencies

There was also evidence of links with planning groups such as community development teams/projects.

Links with private sector organizations were mentioned less by family centres in the study, although specific projects could attract potential sponsors. For example, an innovative project by one family centre, involving internet access to support services by children and young people, had attracted the interest of British Telecom as a potential sponsor:

> We have a bit of a link with the private sector. So far as it goes – and again, this is all quite new but BT are quite interested in our website bits and are interested in supporting that. Also, the local Chamber of Commerce people find themselves at the beginning of the year with money that they have and are not entirely sure what to do with it. So we've built up a link with a group called Splash, that's a combination of the local Chamber of Commerce; and we're looking at getting some money from them to sponsor our after-school programme.

How did other agencies view their links with family centres?

Having looked at links from the perspective of the centres themselves we wanted to explore the views of those agencies with whom they worked. In other words, we wanted to look down the other end of the telescope.

Each family centre in our interview sample of 40 was asked to provide information about three key agencies with whom they worked. These agencies were contacted and asked to comment on the helpfulness of these links for either themselves or the families with whom they worked. It was noticeable that nearly four fifths of other agencies, 79 per cent, described positive outcomes for their own organizations from having links with family centres. No agency said there were negative outcomes from linking with family centres.

On a personal basis, other agencies reported opportunities for:

- developing better understanding of behaviours exhibited by parents and of family dynamics
- developing social and community links and increasing knowledge of local resources
- developing skills and experience

- reflecting on their own practice
- accessing support for themselves.

In terms of the overall provision of services, agencies reported positive outcomes, including:

- a varied and flexible service provided by family centres, with a willingness to experiment, offering realistic packages of services on a group and individual basis, encompassing child protection, family-based and community-oriented work
- clear decision-making, review and evaluation of the progress of services
- specialist programmes of work and the development of new services to support parents having problems such as drug and alcohol abuse, mental health, parenting issues
- an holistic approach, with greater emphasis on preventive measures, based on regular attendance by families
- group sessions and individual work.

In terms of specific services, these agencies reported positive outcomes including high-quality, improved assessments, quality day care/early nursery provision within smaller group settings, and planned placements.

Agencies reported that, through their links with family centres, there were opportunities for increased and improved collaborative working and inter-agency interactions. They commented on the positive approach to joint planning and delivery of family support services, and how this actively broke down barriers to joined-up working and facilitated seamless services. In particular, it engaged more agencies in the child protection process.

Other agencies also felt there were opportunities for mutual exchanges of referrals and provision of services to people who otherwise would be unlikely to access or accept support. Through their relationships with families, family centres were in a position to identify at an early stage potential child protection issues and medical needs. Parents who were not previously known to social workers, and would not otherwise have been offered support, could be linked into family centre services. In the same manner, parents lacking basic skills could be linked into educational support. Centres with open access policies, which also emphasized a willingness to accommodate families if at all possible, were seen as responding more readily than statutory bodies, so contributing to the prevention of crises.

Links with family centres were felt to afford opportunities for workers to share concerns, information, knowledge, perspectives, resources, skills, good practice, and responsibility. And, on this basis, family centres helped agencies improve communication and the understanding of respective and mutual roles. Working together in terms of developing a complementary approach to services could, it was felt, avoid gaps and duplication and provide complementary skills and continuity of support. For example, family centres could take children as they became too old for Sure Start and could provide crèche facilities to support courses and groups.

Workers in other agencies who were positive about family centres perceived family centre staff as sources of advice and support, inspiring confidence, being reliable. They were noted for their commitment, helpfulness, range of skills, enthusiasm, friendly attitude and good interpersonal skills. As one social worker put it, 'They've never let me down'.

This positive view was not shared by everyone. Eighteen per cent of other agency workers, the majority of which were in social services departments, thought links with family centres were only marginally successful for their organizations and 3 per cent thought they were not successful at all. When articulated, negative observations on links with family centres for organizations tended to refer to the fact that, on both sides, there could be a lack of understanding arising from very different approaches to the provision of services. There were also difficulties in the agency and centre finding a convenient time to meet, or for the agency to find time to attend family centre reviews. In most of these cases, the underpinning problem was a lack of formal systems of communication. These problems are explored in more detail in the next chapter.

From the perspective of these agencies, who took a rather more negative view of family centres, prioritization of child protection work was sometimes felt to limit the availability of other services, particularly for children with special needs. We found a general perception on the part of these external agencies that family centres gained more from links with them than vice versa.

The advantages of links with others for children and families

As important as describing the range and nature of links is estimating how productive or otherwise these links turned out to be for all of the stakeholders. Our intensive study of 40 centres showed that 87 per cent of 'other agency' workers viewed their links with family centres as successful for their children and families. Overall, family centres were seen as providing an intensive form of support in terms of contact time and the development of relationships between workers and parents. This was particularly appreciated by health visitors.

The success of family centres was associated with the degree of *accessibility* they offered children and parents. Family centres that were community-based were seen to provide easy access, a *one stop shop service*, within the community. This, in combination with family centres' links with other service providers, such as mental health services, could 'fast track' families to appropriate services.

Other agencies also referred to 'success' in terms of the *acceptability* of family centre services. Agencies told us that parents might have concerns about judgemental attitudes, confidentiality and the involvement of social services. However, in family centres, 'one step removed from social services', agencies felt families were more likely to experience an impartial approach, which enabled them to access help and advice in a non-threatening environment, from suitably experienced and trained workers. Through this, it was felt that parents might become 'more relaxed in the company of professionals'. Active groups run by service users further allowed parents to participate in planning and service provision.

In terms of safeguarding children, other agencies reported, as a positive outcome, the prevention of family breakdown and care proceedings, through clear assessment and provision of early and appropriate support so that children could remain at home.

Summarizing the other agency workers' perceptions of positive outcomes for children, parents and families, the following points were important:

The advantages of family centres for *children* included:

- engagement of children who fall between services and whose needs could often go unrecognized

- a child-centred and child-friendly approach: better understanding of children's issues, their feelings and wishes, by workers skilled in direct work with children

- quality day care for children, particularly for children who otherwise could be difficult to place

- enhanced child development in terms of: health, mental health, education, life skills, personal/social development; happier, well-adjusted children

- support in dealing with family stress

- formal assessment, including future educational needs

- improved safety of children

- individual care planning

- successful placements

- youth projects and structured activities for young people.

Other agency workers' perceptions of advantages for *parents* included:

- access to advocacy, information and support, particularly for parents having special needs such as learning disabilities

- opportunities to develop social and support networks, making links with other parents experiencing similar problems

- empowerment to take responsibility for their children through a partnership approach

- development of coping skills and strategies for improved parenting and management of children's behaviour and increased awareness of children's needs

- personal development, improved self esteem, confidence and independence; opportunities for making personal recovery and changes, for example through counselling, beneficial to themselves and their children

- having a break from home and children.

Respondents' perceptions of advantages for *families* included:

- an holistic approach

- provision of a range of appropriate, planned and co-ordinated services, on a short-term or regular basis, based on assessment of families' needs

- improved family life and dynamics; alleviation of stress; reduction in risk of child neglect or abuse

- improved housing and the physical environment; reduction in evictions

- social inclusion: 'rhetoric of inclusion is beginning to take effect'

- support for children's transition to school.

What can the experience of family centres of working in partnership contribute to the development of children's centres?

In this chapter we have explored in depth the way in which family centres develop and sustain links with other agencies, and how they forged operational partnerships. If these challenges were important at the millennium, they have become even more prominent since 2003. We can identify several relevant messages for the post-2003 period.

First, our study underlines the importance of making an explicit commitment to partnership in respect of developing centre-based provision in the community. This principle has been true of family centres, and is likely to apply just as strongly to children's centres. Making this commitment explicit gives a very clear message to other agencies about the value of partnership. In the light of any anxieties or misapprehensions that local stakeholders may hold about the likely impact of children's centres on their work, this commitment will be even more crucial.

Some possible partners may need a more persistent approach and some professional groups, for example, GPs, may be particularly difficult to engage. It is clear from our findings that one key lesson overshadows all the others in terms of the partnership task: no one agency can construct a partnership on its own! All the stakeholder agencies including family centres and children's centres need to seize every opportunity for establishing and developing partnerships with each other. These overtures and alliances may be made in the context of funding transactions, developing agreed referral procedures, or working together with new community-based initiatives such as Sure Start. Children's centres need to be as inclusive in their own approaches to local stakeholders as we found family centres to be.

Individual areas will have inherited different historical attitudes to collaboration. We found that geographical proximity between partners and family centres facilitated partnership. Where centres shared a building with others, this maximized the possibility of good collaboration and partnership working, a characteristic that has implications for planning decisions now. This does not mean that merely co-locating in one building will automatically generate good partnership working. Partnerships will only come about and flourish if people work to make them happen.

We learned from the study that some links were especially useful. Where a family centre was seen as closely allied to child protection work, there were advantages in such centres cultivating partnerships with other family support agencies, to counterbalance any possible stigma which might otherwise deter families from coming to the centre. Personal links between staff from family centres and those from different agencies were a powerful force in building mutual trust and genuine partnerships. These insights are likely to be as relevant whether the centre in question is a family or children's centre. In other words, it is essential that the National Child Care Strategy and the *Every Child Matters* agenda be integrated with each other. Supportive services for parents, including good quality day care, should not be seen as reflecting different values from those spelt out in *Every Child Matters*.

Chapter 4

Family Centres and Social Services

Tensions and Opportunities

This chapter focuses on what is perhaps the central relationship within which family centres develop and deliver their services. This is their relationship with social services departments. The relationships forged between social services and family centres can be transposed into the forging of links within the new departments of children's services and the new children's services authorities. Much can be learned from the experience of family centres.

As we have shown in the last chapter, 81 per cent of family centres took referrals from social services departments and for this, as well as other reasons that we will discuss in this chapter, social services are clearly of considerable significance for family centres. This chapter seeks to provide an overview of the working relationships between the family centres and the social services departments in our study. It shows that working together between family centres and social services is a complex undertaking, which is complicated by many professional and organizational challenges. Family centres' own descriptions of their specific interactions with mainstream social services were closely related to how they saw their relationship in more general terms. If family centres perceived themselves to be providing services to children and families as *an integral part of* social services or *on behalf of* social services, this was frequently associated with a positive relationship between the two. If a different model was in place, the relationship could be more complex.

The chapter is divided into three sections. First, we identify five specific challenges to the process of working together, some of them clearly more substantial than others. These issues are not unfamiliar ones and have tended to recur in much of the literature on partnership working (Balloch and Taylor 2001; Glendinning *et al.* 2002). Second, we describe the strategies family centres have adopted to overcome these tensions, and finally we review the extent to which family centres can be seen to be maintaining their inheritance.

Five specific challenges to the process of working together

In some cases, we found that family centres and mainstream social services could operate almost completely separately, irrespective of any organizational links in place. As a consequence they were largely unable to appreciate each other's ways of working. At the heart of this 'chasm' lay a set of issues, including different sets of priorities, differing levels of qualifications and experience, and different roles in the assessment process. The source of such 'tensions' was predominantly but not exclusively the formal organizational roles set by their agencies. We now explore them briefly one by one.

Differing sets of priorities

Respondents across both family centres and social services departments cited the issue of different priorities as a major factor in their different perspectives. Such differing priorities could prevent both sets of workers from always understanding the respective pressures for their peers in the other organization. One family centre manager told us:

> We tend to get on with the work that we're doing and we're not affected. When they're really busy, we're not particularly affected by that. On the other hand, when we're really busy, they can be completely unaware of that.

Family centre staff tended to distinguish between the limitations of the organization itself and the individual workers with whom they had contact. Whilst clear statements of expectations were available within social services' documents, including service level agreements, in reality the nature of the referrals made, and the work required of the centres, reflected the attitudes and personalities of individual social workers and managers. This could clearly work positively for the centre, as one manager said:

> I think there's been a lack of communication for a while with social services, but it is getting better. They have a new manager who has more of an understanding of where we're coming from.

However, the attitude of social work managers could also have a negative impact. The findings from interviews with social services and family centre staff suggested that tensions could arise from interactions at an individual level between family centre staff and mainstream social workers. These sometimes related to an absence of liaison. As one manager of a family centre put it:

> Some social workers share our view of the need to work as a team with the family. Others, once they've done the initial assessment, will come to us and ask for feedback but they're not heavily involved with the family. Others will refer on to us and close the case. It may not be the way we want to work – they're doing their bit and we're doing our bit. There's very little sort of liaison about that, which is not the ideal situation really.

Where it occurred, this lack of liaison and mismatch of priorities could sometimes reduce the effectiveness of some specific types of work. Restoring children home from the looked-after system was seen by several respondents as a particularly vulnerable area if liaison was flawed. Because plans for the child necessitated sensitive and timely feedback after supervised contact sessions, gaps in communication between staff prejudiced the prospects for the child's successful return home. At the very least, delays in such communication put back the original timetable:

> It's not good for the child to be in that sort of limbo position. It's more about personalities, caseloads, being busy and sick leave than the interests of the child. Some social workers come in, read the notes, then pop down and make sure the family are OK and everything is on course. Others see it very much, 'Oh! they're at the family centre today. That's covered'. So they'll go and do a visit on another day. It's whether you work together or in parallel that makes a difference.

Beyond these tensions at the individual level, we also found some inconsistency or lack of clarity around roles and responsibilities. Sometimes, as this comment from a social worker shows, social services departments were unsure as to what was expected of family centres:

> We need some clarity about what family centres are really supposed to be doing. I'm quite attracted to the idea of the big open door but there have to be some boundaries around it as well as what other teams are going to be picking up and when and how. We should start off from the point of actually being clear what the family centre should be doing and maybe have some agreed model.

A further issue was the frustration felt by centre managers when their requests for help were not given priority by social services. Whereas the work of mainstream agency social workers with families was often dominated by their statutory duties towards children in need of protection and the management of crisis situations, family centres saw themselves responding to families in a more rounded way. As one manager explained, tensions could develop where social services' organizational concerns were perceived to impede the individual and preventive approaches of family centres to families' needs:

> We have now sent off maybe four copies of this referral – not about abuse – and nothing's been done and we know we're looking at a child at risk. Social services are busy. I wouldn't do their job – I left statutory work because of how it was. But I have to be aware of the client and sometimes I know we appear to be 'precious' to social services because we're going on about this case when they have maybe 50 of the same cases on duty.

It was, however, the mismatch in priorities between 'prevention' and 'protection' that encapsulated the differences between the respective agency remits. Working in a family centre was associated with a more positive, optimistic approach to helping children and families. Family centres were able to adopt an approach that built on the strengths of children and families. In many cases, managers themselves set the tone for a positive and respectful approach to families coming into the centre. Several family centre managers highlighted the importance of approaching the task of assessment in a strengths-based style, as these two examples show:

> One thing that people say to me is 'Your staff are always quite optimistic' and I think that they are. They like to believe the best. We know it doesn't always happen but because we start from the point that it can work out, I think it does make it easier to work with families. We look at the strengths of the families, which is crucial. I think social work does get so entrenched sometimes that 'everybody's a problem', because that's what they get presented and you can get to feel like you just deal with the problems without looking at the potential of individuals as well.

> I think that we try to balance up the strengths and weaknesses. When social workers go out on an investigation or an injury, which is the first thing you've got to look at, the injury becomes the priority. When we come to work with the family, we're looking at effecting change. It's also important to believe that it can happen. Sometimes it doesn't, but if you're coming from a positive mindset, you'll work at it. If you are a social worker you're constantly looking at abuse and nothing else, and only seeing that. We look for the families' strengths.

Clearly, family centre managers and workers were confident of their abilities to provide relevant expertise and services for children and families, given a degree of autonomy or at least a minimum of restraints from social services. However, in order to maximize the opportunities for families and children, they felt it was important to work alongside social workers and build good relationships. This helped increase the effectiveness of their work and the sustainability of their family centre services:

> We are their resource. And you can go and talk to them and I am absolutely confident they will say they could not have survived without us being here and the service they get is first class. They've got no complaints about us, which is remarkable. That's what I aim for all along. I always say to my team, 'Think of us as a business. The people who are buying our goods are the social services therefore the social workers must be treated with the utmost dignity and respect and care because they're the people who will support us when the time comes to examine whether we should exist or not'. So that's our attitude to the social workers. We get cross with them sometimes because sometimes their practice is a bit negative and we have to point it out to them. But on the

whole, we've got a very good working relationship with them. And the team members have direct contact with the social workers.

Having explored some of the issues involved in individual and personal relationships, we now turn to some of the differences on a practical and professional level between centre and social services' staff. These could sometimes, though not always, be the source of tensions.

Differing levels of qualification and experience

Often, family centre workers in the study had been involved in mainstream social services work with children and families for a number of years, and had pursued professional development through a range of training courses in addition to their lengthy work experience. Their views, based on their own extensive experience and training, could conflict with the views of mainstream social workers, particularly those who were relatively inexperienced in direct work with children:

> We get brand new social workers who don't understand. These are new workers coming in who don't know what the policies and procedures are, even things like why they're here for a core group. They get very defensive when, as a family centre manager, I try to assist them and say 'I'm the key worker!' It's very difficult and very frustrating because it could work really well. I think the tension lies mostly in the child protection referrals where the case is open and there has been some keywork, but it's very poor. We take it on and do lots of good work but passing it back can create tension.

A recurring issue for centre staff was the short period of time over which the social workers with whom they worked had been professionally qualified. This concern also extended to the social services managers:

> We're speaking to people who have only been qualified for two years – if that – and it gets even more difficult if they're being supervised by people who haven't been supervisors that much longer.

Diversity of experience was not always seen as a negative factor, either by family centre or social services staff. We found instances where different viewpoints were accepted as a positive aspect of collaborative working, and even, in some cases, where their value was specifically acknowledged in the service level agreements:

> We don't always agree with each other – I wouldn't like – we've just been in big-time dispute professionally about – the local authority took a care order and I didn't think they should have done. So it's not collusive and we have professional disagreements. The local child protection manager is very keen that there should be a difference of view and that people should feel comfort-

able expressing their own – if you want your difference in view minuted at conference, that's fine as well!

Professional mistrust could go both ways. Family centres were sometimes felt by social workers not to understand the scope and ethos of the work they themselves were undertaking, in spite of the pressures on them from management to focus mainly on assessment and care management.

Some family centre staff considered their own professional development to be superior to that of field social workers, in that they were not so regularly subjected to the negative impact of organizational changes and pressures. One social worker based in a family centre commented:

> Constant changes and also the endless process of being distracted on to certain issues is stressful. They [the area social workers] try to settle to do one particular piece of work or process and then they're distracted by someone else's child protection investigation. Tensions and pressures that are experienced in the fieldwork team feed directly through to us. We can get knocked out of shape sometimes – and that takes quite a bit of holding on to and we don't always succeed.

Apart from the difference in professional experience, a further tension related to the formal allocation of roles as between social workers in the context of the purchaser/provider split. This resulted in separating individuals into case managers and those who worked with children and families. It was seen as particularly damaging to the skills of newly qualified social workers who had never had experience of a more integrated approach to social work which they could use to temper their current roles and tasks. This system resulted in some social workers being deprived of direct work experience or having no case management experience, including deciding what services they would commission. This truncated experience had implications for their willingness to shoulder responsibility for the outcome of some of the decisions they made.

By contrast, family centre workers perceived a freedom and flexibility in their own work, including a positive sense of their own professional authority, which could contribute to more effective outcomes for families:

> Not to decry the social workers at all – they've got an incredibly hard job and they're always at the receiving end of criticism, abuse whether it be from other agencies or the public. ... And I'm sure I did it myself when I was in fieldwork. Even your language – you are so careful about how you say things that you stop talking in plain English and I think we have the advantage of being able to talk plainly. If they've got a really horrendous situation, there was a time when I'd have said to a certain family, 'If you don't get this house cleaned up, I am going to go to court to talk about whether we can remove your children. So do you understand that?' Now you won't get social workers saying that these days but they'll skirt round it so much that all they do is infuriate the families who think, 'What is it that they're saying?' Now, I feel in my role, I

can say to families, 'If you don't clean it up you might have to go to court' but they use words like 'may have to seek legal advice'. Well, it's skirting round it.

Family centre workers did acknowledge that they often enjoyed more facilitative working environments. They had totally different functions because they did not carry cases or the responsibility of decision-making at the end of the assessments. So they acknowledged their role was a 'bit of a luxury'. They had the opportunity to take an in-depth look at what was happening in a family and consider the problems from all angles. Such work was felt to be satisfying and enjoyable because, although keeping a child safe was always there in the background, there was little child abuse investigation. Family centre workers appreciated that such work could be demanding and painful. While family centre workers had some child protection work, they also had the luxury of seeing the children benefiting from groups and the way in which children with special needs could blossom.

Differential roles in the assessment process

There were some differences about the power accorded to social workers and family centre staff when it came to making decisions. A small number of family centre respondents explained they might well be excluded from decision-making and networking if their opinion was at variance with that of social services social workers. We found the following statement in the annual report of one family centre:

> There have been a number of occasions where our assessment of a family is at odds with the social worker's view. We then find we stop receiving invitations to meetings or other agencies are approached to begin the assessment again.

Some family centres coped with these challenges in a subtle but strategic way. Rather than have an explicit disagreement about the plan for an individual child, in which they would risk being over-ruled, they sought to 'guide' referrers to a more accurate assessment of the child's needs. They might also take the opportunity to broaden out the focus of intervention. Several centre staff commented along the same lines, believing they were better at seeing the needs of the parents at the same time as the needs of the child, as this example shows:

> One classic was a referral which said that this lady's husband died of cancer, second husband set fire to himself, the third husband is beating her, and the children are very disturbed. The social worker said the mother was having trouble handling the children's behaviour. I said, 'I think actually this lady needs something for herself before we go into that!' There were times when you could fall out with them but we've chosen not to. We've chosen to maintain a good working relationship with them for the sake of the families and also for our future, because they buy our services. But we are open to the

general public so we've got that constant balance of folk coming in off the street and referrals from social services.

Specific structural and bureaucratic issues

The internal divisions generated by the purchaser–provider split in the delivery of social services, which has continued to be a feature of many local authorities since the early 1990s, could further complicate relationships between social workers as *purchasers* and family centre staff as *providers*. In the context of a requirement within social services for the separation of purchasers and providers of services, attempts by family centres to network with mainstream social services, and to familiarize potential and actual referrers with their work, put them in the position of contravening the norms of the internal market in social services.

In addition, social workers, in their role as purchasers of services, sometimes failed to consult with centre staff and gave the impression they rather arrogantly assumed the role of the family centre was simply, as one centre manager put it, 'to be there to meet their own requirements'. This applied especially in cases where attendance at a family centre was seen as part of care planning:

> Social workers are quite happy going to court but they've got to come up with a plan. And they put us on it without even asking! And then they come back and say, 'Well it's under the court now! You have to give us a place', without even asking if we have any places.

Further, family centre staff felt that social workers saw family centres as 'just another service they could purchase'. One family centre worker we spoke to had recently had a particularly depressing experience:

> One social worker in the team sees family centres as there to fill the gap, just as yet one more thing. When we were leaving after the meeting last week, I asked her, 'Why do you feel as a team we are just a commodity ... and you don't see us as anything in our own right that can actually do the same work?' I didn't get an answer.

Many family centres had service level agreements with social services. The actual monitoring of service agreements by social services varied. There were two main frustrations for family centres. These were the irony of more casual relationships causing frustrations and uncertainty and predictable resentment at an overly rigid set of arrangement for monitoring. The disadvantages included getting feedback about services and the renegotiation of the service level agreement:

> When I first arrived I had a much more rigorous relationship with social services – we had three monthly meetings, I sent stats in to them. Now – I don't know if it's because I've been here for a while or they've decided we're

all right or they're busy doing other things, but I don't get that sort of feedback any more at all. And renegotiating the service level agreement is taking forever. Ridiculously so! We haven't technically got a proper one as yet, although we're under discussion and have been for two years. And they think they've got on with us and they're still giving us the money. I think they're happy with us. It's not because there are any problems it's because they're actually looking at their other problematic areas perhaps or something like that.

Sometimes, the laid-back nature of the arrangements was serious enough to delay the renewal of service agreements. Not having a current agreement tended to generate anxiety on the part of centre managers, even if, in reality, no negative consequences ensued:

We should have, but the last one that was physically signed was five years ago. I had a 'phone call yesterday to say that they're going to do a review and hopefully we'll have a new agreement. I'm not really worried in one sense because what I'm doing is part of our service level agreement. This is supposed to steer the pattern that we work to in terms of the work we do. But if you were to look at the last one we drew up, it is totally out of date to what we're doing now, for instance.

In spite of the positive examples of a relatively relaxed approach, not withstanding the frustrations involved, the study overall identified an emerging national trend towards tighter controls over family centres to ensure priority targeting around staffing, to meet financial constraints and the targets set by initiatives like Best Value and Quality Protects. We found evidence of moves toward increasingly tight control in relation to both social services' and voluntary sector family centres:

We are part of social services so that gives us some boundaries in terms of thresholds. And those thresholds are increasing at the moment in terms of whereas sort of five years ago we would have been doing a lot of family support work, working with parents on behaviour management, potty training – just general child development issues. That's moving away now into more child protection issues.

We've just had an assessment by the local authority and they kind of time managed us – asked us what we did with our time. We came out OK in that. They're watching us. They're getting their pounds-worth – they really are but so far we haven't heard about getting it cut. I mean if they did cut us, it would get so difficult that we couldn't function. I think if they cut us that would be the end of us. We're on a minimum budget at the moment.

Family centres were sympathetic to what drove the tightening up of management. They acknowledged the limited budget with which social services struggled and that the departments were constantly being expected to respond to new policy directions from government.

Geographical location

Geographical location was sometimes a source of tension. There was a tendency in some authorities for a marked geographical separation between social services' family centres and the 'mainstream' of the organization. This sometimes had historical roots in that social services departments had needed to seize the opportunity to take on premises as and where they could. In one or two cases, a family centre might be sited in a completely isolated position. One family centre, for example, was based in a huge detached house in its own two acres of ground. This geographical isolation sometimes resulted in centres being 'overlooked' and 'marginalized' unless they continually promoted their services. Geography put a premium on pro-activity but there was no doubt that distance could be overcome, with difficulty, by active intra-agency networking:

> We do have some difficulties because all of the rest of children and families' teams are on another site and so they sometimes feel quite distanced from us whereas before we used to work on lots of different sites and so everyone had to make an effort to communicate and liaise really closely. And I think because they don't see us on a day-to-day basis they can feel a bit apart from that. But on the whole, we're involved in everything that goes on within children and families' teams.

Where family centres and social workers were fortunate enough to be located near each other and had the will to work together, perceptions were particularly positive:

> I think what's happened is we work really well here, with the social work team, we've got a good relationship – we go out and do joint assessments, we talk to each other. It's not like some of the others who say that social workers will never ring them back. It's brilliant! The other side of the city doesn't work very well because the social work teams are in separate offices. In fact, they're six miles down the road from each other and quite a way from the nearest family centre. So, it's hardly surprising there isn't that much rapport between the social work teams, never mind with us.

Strategies for minimizing tension

As we have indicated earlier, the source of tensions for family centres often lay outwith the control of the respective sets of workers. However, some family centres developed a considerable capacity and expertise in managing social workers' involvement. In doing so, workers often had to balance the views of the social worker and the family:

We've got a much more comprehensive referral form than we used to have. And social services are supposed to identify quite clearly on what they expect the family to get when they come here. In addition to that there's a slot for the families to say what they would hope to get from coming here. Once that referral has been agreed we set up a three-way meeting between the referrer, the family and ourselves. So we can discuss openly what is in everyone's best interests. And if you're doing a formal assessment, that three-way meeting is particularly crucial. At the end of the assessment process, you don't end up with social services saying to us 'You said you were going to do that' or 'We thought you were going to do that'. And we ensure we record what we have agreed, as in the past we've been put in a position where people had expected us to do things that we had not agreed to do.

Although they were both pursuing the same goal of the best outcome for children and their families, we found family centre workers sometimes felt they needed to 'educate' fieldwork teams so that they were aware of the contribution of family centre work. Far from being seen as a mere advertisement for themselves, in many instances respondents described this activity within the context of their professional responsibilities.

Mobility in the workforce constituted a further dimension to the necessity of doing the work of advertising what they had to offer. One manager went so far as to describe this professional activity as being akin to 'painting the Forth Bridge – you just get to the point where they all know about the centre, then it's all change and you have to start all over again':

Staff move in and out of social work so often here that people don't have an understanding of what we do. We constantly do presentations to teams about what we can do and what we can't do really, and we do it regularly so that, as new faces come in, they will have access to what the rest of the team know.

In spite of these challenges, family centre workers were proud of the work they did in its own right, based on a clear family support philosophy and not merely as a subsidiary element to field social work. They expected field social workers, who were sometimes seconded to them or who had elected to work in the centre, both to appreciate their approach and to sign up to this way of working:

There are some quite large overlaps really but, I suppose, particularly in the last two or three years, we've been quite actively trying to influence a change of practice, to change the way they look at referrals and handle things in the fieldwork team. The skill base for direct work with children is much stronger in family centres than it is in fieldwork teams. For a lot of fieldwork teams that's been lost or eroded but we expect them to engage in direct work if they come here. A social worker working in a family centre is no good to us if they want to behave like a field worker. They might as well go down the road and practice fieldwork.

Sometimes, the expectations that their work would be valued were not fulfilled. Some family centre staff found the absence of a sense of professional solidarity between themselves and the area teams disappointing and disheartening. Social workers within social services sometimes failed to acknowledge the contribution of family centres to the overall work of their departments. Family centre staff felt that social workers in social services departments saw themselves as 'professional' social workers but regarded family centre staff as something rather different, even though family centre workers were often undertaking mainstream activities, such as direct work with children and families, which have been traditionally regarded as the core of social work activity. Additionally, the failure of social workers to appreciate the role of observation of children and families within their ordinary daily routines was, at best, short-sighted.

One centre manager recounted her experience:

> We do a camping holiday every year, very cheap and I go with the families. I take my family. A social worker asked me what taking families on holiday has got to do with social work. Which is quite an interesting comment. I actually photocopied the part of the Children Act about holidays for families being encouraged, and how families should be helped to make sure that they get a holiday. You can pick up so much about family dynamics if you see them in a different setting. They could go into a social work unit and behave perfectly for an hour or not perfectly for an hour but be with them for a whole week and you see the whole microcosm, including the problem behaviour of both parents and children.

In order to counteract social workers' misconceptions of family centres, family centre managers painted a vivid picture of the strategies they adopted to overcome these tensions and build sound relationships. These included:

- designating a link worker in the family centre who took primary responsibility for developing and sustaining the overall link
- inviting social workers to open sessions
- poster campaigns which portrayed the centre's activities and could be displayed in area offices
- a telephone hotline with a named individual to facilitate the two-way flow of information.

Maintaining the family centre inheritance

One important factor that emerged from the study in the relations between social services and family centres was of a set of high expectations on the part of social services and of a wide range of work undertaken by family centres in response. In optimum conditions this did not pose a problem, and family centres took pride and pleasure in the breadth and distinctiveness of the work they could undertake. If relationships were good, any necessary negotiations could be undertaken amicably to arrive at an agreed plan of work even though this might be extensive, as this example shows:

> What they [social services] do is refer cases through to us for us to work with and that's a whole range from risk assessments directly with the children – we work with children they suspect have been abused but there's been no disclosure ....We've actually done bereavement counselling for children. The latest one they've asked us to do is working with a family where a Schedule One offender's coming into the home, having been found guilty of sexual offences against children and we designed our own programme of working with the family which is working with children, with the mother, with the perpetrator. And so the range of what we do for social services is quite enormous, including handling children's behaviour.

Where arrangements worked well, even if family centres had local and service level agreements with social services, they were allowed considerable flexibility in how they implemented the work:

> We have to work with 40 families on an individual basis but we don't have to have a percentage of those that are child protection. The reality is that about a quarter of them are child protection cases but that goes in waves. It can be more, it can be less. So, we're not having to do comprehensive assessments and things. While doing assessment is on our service level agreement, how we implement them – that is our choice.

One centre provided the example of being able to run a group for boys who had been referred because of challenging behaviour. They realized that they were being asked to concentrate solely on the boys rather than looking at the child within the family system, which they felt would not be effective. Within their flexible working practices, they were able to decide to run the boy's group alongside a group for their parents. This worked well, with good outcomes for both children and parents. The centre staff commented that this was an example of how they had the scope to develop and try things out. They felt they were not forced to work in a certain way. They could incorporate the kinds of work that social services asked them to do within the framework of their own service system.

Another way of overcoming challenges occurred where, despite the fact that family centres were often heavily reliant on local authority funding, there seemed still to be scope to accommodate individual priorities and different ways of working:

> We have a service level agreement with the local authority which determines the level of work they expect from us. It's linked to certain grants that we get each year. It's probably about half the amount of money we get now but

nevertheless it's the reliable money, the money we know we're going to get so it gives us the opportunity to develop structures. So it's obviously quite significant … because we're actually working to their priorities a lot of the time. However it's not entirely that because we can do a certain amount of day care sessions for children. They also allow us to do some community group work and take self referrals as well which I think is quite good. In fact if you look at our referrals … self referral is one of the highest forms of referrals that we actually get. But that's allowed for on the service level agreement.

In some cases, centres could easily meet social services' minimum requirements because they were given the flexibility to do so:

They've been remarkably loose with the service level agreement. I'm quite surprised. What they're advocating is six families per family centre so we would guarantee to work with twelve families at any one time. I mean it doesn't work … people don't just come in on a regular basis which actually means we only need three families in on the referred day and the two referred days in each centre. If I was fully staffed, I would be aiming for four families so that you've always got one – it might be a bit tight if they all turned up but in the main you're going to get one who's off so you keep up the numbers, you keep up the staff motivation, keep up the dynamics of the group of people coming too. They haven't stipulated that that's just for the family centre so the fact that we've now got the outreach, the outreach worker usually works with three families so we've got that picked up as well. So it's quite loose in terms of the work that we do.

If overall we found widespread evidence of a set of relationships in which individuals did their best to overcome the challenges which political, organizational and professional imperatives posed, there was one area where challenges remained. It was impossible to ignore the enduring nature of the tension for both agencies to balance prevention and protection. In spite of the refocusing debate which followed the Department of Health's review of child protection services in 1995 (Department of Health 1995), we found that there had been little shift in the balancing of 'protection' and 'prevention' at the overall social services level. For example, the balance between early and late intervention family support services could represent a major source of tension between family centres and mainstream social services. We found that mainstream social services were still highly likely to prioritize crisis child protection enquiry work and associated intensive or specialized services. Family centres, whether or not they were part of social services, generally acknowledge the value of a broader approach, and for the most part, prioritized accessible and preventive services at an early stage in the identification of need. The dilemma and challenges were well expressed by one centre manager:

Where do we stand? Because we're not the child protection end. We don't take your kids away, you know as people fear. We are still within social services but working as we do with communities, sometimes we're seen as a bit soft. I worked for many years in child protection, looked after children and I know it's a very difficult job. I wouldn't deny that for one minute! And I think if you're in it, you actually don't see the value of working in a much broader way which we do here, I hope.

With their emphasis on prevention, family centres wished to protect what they saw as very valuable direct work with children and parents. Consequently, there was reluctance, even in social services' family centres, to succumb to the pressure from social services to take the burden of the acute assessment work:

I think the tension for social services department is that they have a lot of assessment work to do and they would like to hand that over to somebody else and ease their load because their resources are limited. I do not mean that in a critical way at all. If I were them, I would be feeling the same. I think for us it's been exacerbated in the sense that another family centre does comprehensive assessments from start to finish which makes it difficult for us to hold on to our principles about preventive work.

This reluctance was no less evident in the voluntary sector, where family centres often had clear views of how they wished to operate:

We're not social services, we're a voluntary project funded by social services. I wanted to make it feel to families that they were receiving a service, as customers. That's where we've been coming from all the time. And by doing that, we empower clients to come into our drop in service but now we also have to have a separate side where we are able to carry out the assessments using the government's framework.

Some family centres felt they were losing the battle to preserve their mission. In this context, there were often concerns that the preventive, community-based approaches of voluntary sector organizations would be swallowed up by service level agreements, as these two examples show:

I think if they said we'd got to do a certain percentage of comprehensive assessments then we'd struggle to keep our credibility within the community because I think you always have to work hard not to have a label of 'social services' or the stigma of welfare.

We have a service level agreement with social services so we have some things that we have to do and occasionally we have to do things we don't want to. For example, we had to cut our family advice sessions from three to two. That was something we felt was an imposition but we had to do it because we are dependent on them for funding.

The undermining of role was often subtle but unremitting. Approaches at management and policy level in local councils reflected the threats family centres felt exposed to from increasing financial and organizational constraints:

> I think with social services, at the moment, things are OK but there is an element of tension between the city council and voluntary organizations, I think. And I don't mean that on a fieldwork level. I think in terms of teams and social workers things are actually, on the whole, fine. There are, sort of, the occasional – the usual gripes – about social workers not returning calls and things, but on the whole we have very good working relationships. I think that where there is a tension is higher up where they're looking much more at resources, et cetera, et cetera, and more in terms of how it meets their needs as a department.

Some voluntary sector family centres had given in and were willing to accede to social services' priorities and be constrained by their service level agreements, even if this undermined their broader inclination towards family support:

> We have referrals from elsewhere but ... our service level agreement has just been redesigned and ... they've actually written in that they [social services] will take priority. But to be truthful, they've always taken priority simply because we had loads and loads and loads of referrals. Children who were separated from their families would be the primary one, asking us to do an assessment for a court. Having said that, we would always try to balance social services' demands with our aim to provide family support. At the moment, though, the criteria would lie heavily with children who were separated or the assessment for courts.

Some service agreements were broad enough to accommodate onslaughts on their remit. In spite of potentially opposing service priorities, compromise could be achieved, with family centres providing the intensive services required by social services' priorities, while balancing these demands with early intervention work as well. Although centres, like this one in the voluntary sector, were holding to their own remit, there was an element of uncertainty about the future:

> Well, first and foremost this centre is run by a voluntary organization. However, it's completely funded by the local authority so we have a contractual arrangement with them. We have a management agreement which does not specify very clearly what the level of service is or should be. Historically, the organization came in with a clear agenda – my organization is here to run a family support type service with a local authority as the child protection service. And me in the middle – I've straddled that really by giving the purchasers what they want, which is a child protection service – they're paying for it and they call the tune! But with their tacit agreement, we can do some family support. And they want some family support at the moment. They know it happens. The agreement is worded fairly vaguely but there's an overall agreement that we're here to meet the needs of children in need. It's as broad as that really. But with priority being given more and more to children

in need of protection, at this stage our agreement doesn't specify what level our services are to be and I am worried we will be pushed along a different route.

What can the experience of family centres contribute to the building and sustaining of relationships with children's services authorities?

This chapter has shown the ups and downs of the relationship between family centres and social services area teams. It has described the frustrations of family centres about not being understood or valued on occasions. It has also outlined how family centres and social services could work well together. The new agenda will mean that the work previously undertaken under the banner of 'the social services department' will now be incorporated into the activities of children's services departments. However, if the terminology has changed, many of the challenges will persist and the findings from the study remain relevant.

Overall, interviews with centre managers and others pointed to the need for changes to organizational structures to improve liaison and co-ordination. This might include incorporating family centre managers as part of central children's services management teams, the joint management of family centre and fieldwork teams and the regular interchange of workers and managers between fieldwork and family centre work. Social work training placements in family centres and the establishment of management structures within a flattened hierarchy were also seen as a way of creating more effective liaison and co-ordination. With good relationships, service agreements and communication, the study findings showed just how positive and responsive family centres could be to the changing needs and demands of social services. Nevertheless, the centres we studied provided a microcosm of tensions generated when policy focuses in one direction. The push towards child protection investigations rather than a broader family support service was tending to narrow the focus of family centre services. Additionally, the changes in the style of social services' management of service agreements posed serious threats to centres maintaining their broader mission.

Family centres provide a clear example of the challenges the new children's services agenda poses for working across organizational divides. The challenges in the new agenda are even more onerous because of the likelihood of a diverse workforce. This will bring together workers from health, education and social services, sometimes located in a single setting. If a mutual awareness of working patterns and good ongoing relationships are to be developed between workers from professional backgrounds working in different or shared settings, communications need to be very clear and take place on a regular basis.

Workforce practices, such as involving personnel in each other's strategies and management systems, all help foster mutual understanding and appreciation of different roles and tasks. In 2006, at the time of writing, the idea of a 'one stop shop' posed by the Audit Commission in the mid 1990s (Audit Commission 1994) still clearly has credibility in co-locating a multi-disciplinary workforce. The message from this study is that, where different parts of the children's services system are located under the same roof, this can be very helpful in breaking down barriers in communication.

We found that there needed to be clear service agreements between social services and family centres. Where agreements depended on goodwill and were too casual, this could cause frustrations and uncertainty about accountability. On the other hand, the agreement should be reasonable and responsive to changes in demands from service users, and have the capacity for ongoing flexibility in the light of such changes. Children's services authorities will need to maintain the same vigilance and flexibility if new partnerships with centre-based agencies, such as children's centres and extended schools, are to work.

In addition, where centre-based provision is commissioned, those being commissioned can learn much from the determination of family centres to retain a breadth of services and not be corralled by the commissioning process into providing a limited range of services. A crucial feature of family centres in the study was that they could take on a wide range of work because the workforce had transferable skills. These were used to good effect with a range of children and their families. It is therefore important that children's services agencies strive to mirror the breadth of provision to be found in family centres and do not allow themselves, for example, to limit their services to only providing day care with a view to getting parents back into the workforce. Any future centre-based children's services provision needs to offer the whole continuum of services to simultaneously safeguard and promote children's welfare in order to achieve the five outcomes of *Every Child Matters*.

Chapter 5

Delivering Services

The Experience of Family Centres

Getting the task of service delivery right is a complex one for any agency and certainly no less so for family centres. This is a central theme in *Every Child Matters* and the volumes of guidance which have followed. In this chapter, we highlight the strenuous efforts made by family centres to maintain their commitment to a broad vision for services. Overall, they maintained this value position in the face of considerable pressures to narrow their vision and service range. These have been described in the previous chapter.

We found that family centres in the study sought to deliver a range of services which met the needs of parents and their children in the local community. Parents' and children's wants and needs varied as did family centres' responses in the context of their own priorities and those of their funders. Parents in the study looked to family centres, not only for direct support with parenting, but also as a means by which they might find help to develop other aspects of their lives. Personal development interventions could range from enhancement of self esteem to the pursuit of educational attainments that could have an impact on employment opportunities.

The majority of parents in the study described themselves as having limited social and support networks, in addition to a general absence of links with members of their extended family or friends. Social isolation featured as a major factor which tended to undermine parents' ability to cope with parenting and affect their children's development. These experiences tended to be associated with one or more of the following:

- moving to a new area

- geographical or emotional distance from, or lack of, extended family

- having more than one pre-school child

- having a mental health problem.

The range of services

A key focus of this study was to explore the capacity of family centres to respond to the needs of families they served and offer a range of services. The Children Act 1989 had stressed the need for such a range of services in terms of timing and intensity of interventions. The Children Act 1989 emphasizes the following concepts:

- the importance of family support, including day care provision, for pre-school and school-age children, and services to support and improve the strengths and skills of parents in their own homes

- family support services not being restricted to families of children at risk of significant harm, or returning home from being looked after

- the importance of an integrated approach and a continuum of services being available to children and families at different times, according to their changing needs

- family centres constituting an appropriate base for the delivery of family support services.

However, at the same time, the implementation process stipulated that it would not be acceptable for an authority to exclude children from access to services, for example, by confining services to children at risk of significant harm which attracts the duty to investigate under Section 47. The definition of children's needs includes physical, emotional, and educational needs according to age, sex, race, religion, culture and language and the capacity of the current carer to meet those needs (see Aldgate and Tunstill 1995).

In this study, as shown in the last chapter, pressures from competing priorities, in the context of finite or diminishing resources and increasing responsibilities, were felt to result in higher priority being afforded to some service user groups, impacting in turn on family centres' role, accessibility and range of services. The next section uses the findings from the study to explore what is on offer to families and the means by which they can or cannot access those services. First, we look at the range of services offered by family centres.

Irrespective of whether they were part of local authority provision or the independent or voluntary sectors, family centres considered the welfare of children and young people to be the central element of their role. Findings from the national survey suggest that the majority of family centres saw themselves as having a broad focus on children in the context of their families. Therefore,

- 81 per cent focused mainly on both children and their parents.

- 14 per cent focused mainly on children and young people.

- only five per cent focused mainly on parents.

Key elements of the family centres' own descriptions of their role, from the national survey, included the enhancement of children's development, the provision of early years education and the safeguarding of children. These objectives were being met either directly, through the interaction of staff and children or indirectly, through the support of parents.

Key concepts flagged up in the family centre documentation on values which we examined emphasized working in partnership with parents, so that children's needs might be met in the context of promoting parental confidence and parental responsibility over and above this commitment; however, the welfare of children remained the principal focus for family centres.

Our data on the activities of family centres indicated that work in family centres could involve:

- the assessment of need
- the enhancement of parenting skills, involving services such as parenting skills training, video analysis of parent–child interactions, play-based learning
- support for parents and children
- counselling
- speech therapy
- activities and opportunities for personal and/or social development such as exercise classes for parents, aromatherapy and cookery classes
- holiday play activities for children, family fun days
- provision of advice and information, on subjects such as welfare rights and housing
- toy libraries
- practical facilities for laundry.

In addition to these services, all family centres sought to make available personal support by having staff available to listen to families' concerns as and when they arose. The function of 'being there' as a resource was cited by many families as an important characteristic of the positive service delivered by family centres.

A mix of services to meet child and family need at different stages

Family centres in both the statutory and voluntary sector stressed their commitment to combining both early preventive work and late or reactive crisis intervention work. The following quotes from workers give a flavour of the way they approached this challenge:

We aim to support families with children under ten years old. Our role includes preventive services as well as assessment and child protection work with a 50/50 split between the two. (*Local authority centre*)

We look to provide a treatment service to abused children as well as providing support services for children and families in need. (*Local authority centre*)

Our task is to provide a mixture of assessment and support services to families of children in need. (*Voluntary sector centre*)

Through partnership with parents, we aim to facilitate opportunities for growth and development for children under five and support for their parents. This is an under-developed and under-resourced area. We also aim, where appropriate, to prevent children needing to be looked after by the local authority. (*Voluntary sector centre*)

At the same time, family centres' descriptions of their role show that overall, they were more likely to specialize in one type of work, as shown in Table 5.1. Family centre staff were asked to classify this work as either early or late intervention. When we explored the types of work within these categories, it emerged that there were some similar activities, although the proportions of activities might vary according to whether it was part of early or late intervention. So, for example, child protection investigation work could be part of early or late intervention but figured more largely in late interventions. By contrast, the concept of acting as a community resource or offering family support services was more likely to be within the category of early intervention. A minority of family centres offered both early and late interventions and were thus able to offer a broader range of services.

Table 5.1 Services offered by family centres (national survey)

Work type emphasis	Percentage of family centres
Mostly late intervention services	59
Mostly early intervention services	34
Mix of early and late intervention services	7

n=415

Detailed analysis of the services (not shown) revealed that significantly more open access family centres were likely to have an early intervention role (82%); and significantly fewer were likely to have a late intervention role (15%), whereas more family centres accessed only by referral were likely to have a late intervention role (81%); and significantly fewer were likely to have an early intervention role (16%).

Family centre managers in the intensive sample suggested that, even in family centres with a highly specified remit to provide late intervention services, a small proportion of early intervention or open/community types of service were sometimes included in the programme simply to reduce stigma and increase acceptability of services. In addition, although there could be external pressures to restrict their work to more intensive, late interventions, in practice, some centres resisted this pressure and continued to provide support to families earlier in the development of need or neglect. However, attempting to mix early and late intervention work highlighted tensions in some cases:

> We are attempting to give a higher profile to preventive work but still have to put child protection first. We are also trying to offer some services via groupwork, such as a behaviour management group or a group on first aid and safety in the home.

The implications for services of pressures towards specialization

In spite of the fact that the balance of the mix of early and late interventions varied between family centres, there was an overall sense that centres were being pushed towards specializing in late statutory intervention at the expense of the preventive work to which they aspired.

For others, there was a cycle of change, some of it welcome, some of it less welcome. This was summed up by one member of staff:

> When I first came, there were rooms for people who wanted their children to mix, people who felt that their children hadn't got their language yet. There was room for all sorts of things to happen. You didn't even have to justify it because there wasn't a measurement. You just had to say, 'I'm sure she'd benefit from it'. It was all whim and it was all child care stuff – there were no programmes, no set patterns and it was very free help. And I wonder about that because you saw the same woman back with the next child and the intervention wasn't planned. Then we went through a 'Let's all have some good group work and let's look at managing change in your family'. Then very, very recently, it's been a question of change of staff skills – containing play, therapeutic play, adult work, adult and child work, family work, themed system work and now we're moving again to the law to do with children in care, the law to do with keeping children safe. So it's very rapid change. I'd say three years have seen us move from a plethora of, 'whatever you want us to be' to 'we're a specialism as much as your doctor or your dentist' and to 'we're a control agency for the state'.

Some family centres were particularly worried about pressures which contrived to reduce or constrain their role, for example, towards services associated with late crisis interventions. In this context, pressures on local authority social services departments, could, in turn, exert pressures on family centres to alter the balance of their work. One social services centre manager exemplified this approach:

> We are part of social services so that gives us some boundaries in terms of thresholds. And those thresholds are increasing at the moment. Five years ago we would have been doing a lot of family support work but that's moving away now into more child protection issues; and the expectation is that those things will be met within the community, by who knows? That's our major problem here. Recently, the borough has employed a consultant who has come and looked at particular community areas and drawn up plans of their strengths and their weaknesses. The borough has now actually decided to fund a community worker, the latest of which is a pre-school community worker, who is hoping to set up things like toy libraries and parenting groups and things. Ironically, these are things that we used to have and have been moving away from which is a shame.

Resisting the pressures

In spite of such pressures, family centres could be proactive in their response by either officially or unofficially retaining a broad approach, as shown in the last chapter. Indeed, it was evident from the study that both family centres who were part of social services, and those in the voluntary sector, were reluctant to lose the preventive work completely. Their reluctance sometimes acted as a catalyst to devising creative ways to deliver existing services and to the development of closer links with other service providers in order to maintain the breadth and range of services appropriate to families with various levels of need.

Accessibility of services

Although the family centres in the study were subject to pressures associated with pushing them towards an exclusive focus on child protection work, we identified a range of other factors which could have an impact on access to centres and their services. In particular, we discovered a range of gate-keeping systems in operation. Some family centres in the national survey described certain restrictions which they applied to their services. To some extent these varied according to whether they were in the statutory or voluntary sectors. These included:

- task-centred time-limited family support to families with children aged 14 years and under (*local authority centre*)

- risk assessments and a limited number of packages of family support (*local authority centre*)

- targeting the most vulnerable children in need of protection and their carers (*local authority centre*)

- offering family support services within a defined neighbourhood of three (adjoining) council estates (*voluntary sector centre*).

In addition, we looked at the mode of access to family centres in the study and classified them as *open, referred* or *mixed*. Table 5.2 shows that overall, more family centres had a mix of open and referred access rather than only open or only referred.

Table 5.2 shows there was a change in patterns of access over the time of the study. Very few family centres (4%) in the follow-up survey were completely open. This was considerably fewer than the 11 per cent in the 1999 national survey. Additionally, more centres were restricted to referred families only (40%) compared with the national survey (34%). Centres with mixed access changed only marginally over the same period.

Table 5.2 Mode of access

Access	Percentage of family centres	
	Review survey (n=344)	National survey (n=415)
Only open	4	11
Access only by referral	40	34
Mixed	56	55
More services for referred families than open access services	25	
Open and referred about the same	19	
More open access services than for referred families	12	

The study findings showed that, even in open access family centres, in the context of limited resources, demand needed to be managed, for example by restricting publicity:

> We've never advertised our services because we'd be inundated and we'd not be able to cope.

This was not true of every family centre. We found examples of creative publicity, the organization of open days and proactive invitations to potential referrers and families.

When we asked parents in the study how they had heard about their family centre, only 10 per cent referred to publicity material. They explained that their main sources of information were health visitors (34%), social workers (28%) and, more rarely, other professionals (5%). Almost a quarter of parents had heard about the centre through talking to their friends and neighbours.

Self referrals

Very few family centres, most of which were open access, accepted referrals from parents directly. Whilst criteria imposed by social services were frequently cited by family centre managers as an explanation for referral patterns, other influences, including the effects of stigma and reactions to the range of services available, also influenced referral patterns:

> Most of our referrals come from the social work team. We do have a few referrals from health visitors maybe. There are very few self referrals now whereas we used to get a lot of people coming in. I think word gets round that we haven't got a nursery so now they don't.

Attending a family centre – an offer you can't refuse?

Discussions with family centre managers and findings from parents indicated that children's and parents' attendance at family centres appeared to reflect a continuum of choice, from no choice through to high choice. The basis on which parents and children attended family centres ranged through the following:

- no choice: compulsory attendance at the insistence of social services and where the alternative would be break-up of the family.

- low to medium choice: attendance that was acceptable to parents and came about as a result of referral, recommendation, introduction, invitation or active encouragement.

- high choice: attendance at the centre which could be said to be 'proactive' and was genuinely sought out by the parent.

Parents who fell into each of these groups had very similar needs, although, in some cases, these needs were articulated by parents themselves while, in other cases, they were formally defined by professionals within the parameters of compulsory measures.

Managers admitted that there were degrees of 'voluntariness' in attendance:

> We have a mixture. Most – I would say about 90 per cent, come voluntarily. And then we have a small percentage where it's under a court order, under a supervision order or something, that they attend a family centre. Well, those ones – they have to come because it's part of a court order. Of the 90 per cent that come voluntarily, there are probably a third of those who are actually having their arm twisted about it! They may choose not to come but what I would say is that once they've started coming, most of them actually then come voluntarily. It's getting them through the door. It's getting them to not be too anxious about what happens here and what goes on. And it's getting them to experience it.

The interviews with parents also indicated that some felt under pressure to attend, having little or no choice. For example:

> The guardian said if I came I could have my mothering assessed and be helped to be a better mum.

> I did not want to come – the social worker made me come – if I had not come I would not have got my children back.

> It was out of our control really.

Others welcomed the opportunity for support:

> I was excited to have some support.

> I was thankful to be able to come.

Opening hours

Opening hours could influence who attended family centres and the services developed in them. Family centres in the study varied in terms of their opening times. There was also variation in the amount of time allocated for individual parents to attend. This could be time-limited or open-ended. Findings from the interview sample indicated that time restrictions had an impact on families' access to family centres. Restricted opening hours could serve to limit accessibility, particularly for working parents. However, this was not the full picture. The review survey data highlighted a trend towards introducing evening and weekend opening. This was particularly helpful to some parents, such as those who went to work, including fathers, and single parents, who would otherwise be alone all weekend.

Flexibility of access in terms of time was deemed by staff to be essential in family centre work. Some family centre managers expressed the view that, while substance misuse was not necessarily synonymous with poor parenting, drug and alcohol misusing parents were often unable to keep appointments or turn up for services on time. In these cases, ease and immediacy of access were essential. Similarly, some parents had such chaotic lives that forward planning was impossible. While centres might identify as one of their aims with families the achievement of a more structured lifestyle, flexibility of access was needed until such change could be achieved.

Some parents in the study attended their family centre several times a week; others once a week or even less frequently. Parents commented that longer hours, more frequent attendance and no closures for holidays would be appreciated; and that they would prefer there to be no waiting period.

Sometimes family centre workers were at odds with their employing agency. Staff could have family-focused priorities rather than adopting the priorities of their organization and sometimes preferred the idea of increasing opening hours to meet families' needs rather than those of the agency:

> The whole of education shut down for fifteen days over Christmas and I said, 'Well we don't want to shut down because those children in care are not going to get contact over that period'. Social services don't have any facilities for contact. They hold it in offices or they book a room here. So I spoke to the staff and I said would people be willing to come in over the Christmas period and get a day back and we'll open up for a few days so parents can see their children. It's a very emotive time. And two or three of them were willing to do that. So we opened up at Christmas but I don't think anybody in education understood what we were doing or why. And social services didn't think that they would need that service until the week before Christmas and then suddenly, we were inundated with requests for it. But it's just thinking through the needs of the children first of all, not particularly those of the department or whatever.

Location of services

Family centres in the study varied in the size of their catchment areas and the site of their service delivery. Location factors could influence who attended family centres and the services developed for them. Some family centres served local families; others served families who came from much further afield as well.

Lack of family centre support was often associated with a general lack of family support services in the area. This was particularly so in rural communities and in areas where local authorities did less to provide supportive, preventive services for children and families. A couple of miles either side of local authority boundaries could make the difference for families between having high or low levels of family support, or for family centres, between having access to high or low levels of funding. When we talked to some of the professionals who had links with family centres, they told us that, while often appreciating the contribution made by their local family centre to family support in one area, they were unhappy about the lack of similar support in other areas in which they worked.

The availability of transport was another factor in accessibility. For families who lived at a distance from their family centre, and were reliant on public transport, access could often be very difficult, if not impossible.

Family centres that had been former day nurseries were also sometimes located in affluent areas. Interviews with staff in these family centres suggested that funding in such areas was likely to be at a low level and family support needs were not being adequately met.

Support facilities were almost entirely absent in some areas, particularly, but not exclusively, in rural communities. Family centres in rural areas, which usually belonged to independent or voluntary sector organizations, sometimes acted as a base for the location and expansion of a range of services and support agencies. For example, a rural family centre in the study, which had developed very little beyond a small crèche and a few adult education classes, was the planned base for social services outreach work, a health visitor clinic and other public sector services, in a multi-agency strategy to make services local for families in the area.

The accessibility of family centre services: the parents' views

Staff whom we interviewed were well aware of the barriers to accessing their centres. However, we felt that it was important to canvass the views of parents themselves who had experienced both facilitators and barriers to access. We wanted to explore the extent to which these had an impact on families.

Facilitators and barriers to access: parents' perspectives

Parents in the study compared their family centres favourably with other support agencies such as social services and schools, in terms of both immediate accessibility and ease of access. They said that, if they needed to talk to someone, there were usually no delays and no appointments needed, and such ease of access was described as helping avoid protracted worrying whilst waiting for an appointment. Another advantage was that the professional was likely to be a familiar figure and was sometimes described as 'a friend', someone to turn to in difficult times:

> If you have got a crisis, there is someone you can see for a chat and a cup of tea. They are there at the end of a telephone.

> It's easier than talking to someone who is a stranger in social services.

> The family centre listens to problems and is unbiased. There's a laid-back, relaxed atmosphere. They bridge the gap between social services and counselling.

> They give you help for extra stress and don't go through all the red tape of a usual professional body. You can drop in. They act as your friend. There is a

gap generally with other professionals (like doctors and health visitors) but the staff are like your friends.

Prior to attending the family centre, 49 per cent of the parents in the study said they had anticipated problems in approaching their family centres but only 36 per cent felt that these problems had actually materialized. Anticipated problems ranged from practical difficulties, such as travelling with young children, to negative reactions from staff if and when they actually got to the centre. The emotions they described included:

- apprehension generated by not knowing what would happen

- reluctance and anxiety about mixing with other people

- fear that staff and other parents would be judgemental

- stigma associated with people knowing they were there because of a child protection concern

- pride and reluctance to admit the need for help

- embarrassment about not knowing how to care for their children

- reluctance on the part of fathers, who saw family centres as an all-female environment

- worry about the sort of people they would meet there including 'drug addicts' and 'child beaters'.

We found evidence that many of these disincentives and anxieties were felt by the parents to be mitigated by supportive attitudes from staff, as the following comments show:

The staff are understanding here. It took a long time to settle in but with support we now come because we want to.

I'm quite shy so it was quite difficult to get to know everyone but they're very friendly here.

To start with I had panic attacks before coming.

Although I'm a bloke, I felt like 'one of the girls' and actually, it's better surrounded by women.

In summary, it was clear that the majority of parents were supported by staff in their initial contact with the centre. Popular strategies adopted by the staff to allay fears included preliminary meetings between families and centre staff. Particularly effective was the practice of using parents who were already attending the centre to reassure the faint-hearted:

I didn't want to do it on my own so one lady did a home visit first – then came and brought me in so I wouldn't chicken out.

I was really pleasantly surprised because I knew the woman round the corner and I never knew she went to the centre. She always seems like such a good mum.

What lessons can the experience of family centres contribute to the delivery of services for children and their families?

Above all, our findings underline the centrality of the commitment and consistency with which family centres engaged with families. The starting point of their relationship was a fundamental respect for families, which they modelled in their policies as well as in their day-to-day interactions with parents.

The study's findings strongly suggest that services should be planned in partnership with parents who, if given the opportunity, can be highly perceptive about their own needs. However, it cannot be assumed that all parents will be equally confident about making explicit their preferences or needs. A range of inhibiting factors may include anxiety about having their parenting ability judged and found wanting; not having English as a first language; and being isolated and lacking transport facilities to enable them to attend centre-based services.

Obvious ways to minimize these obstacles include a range of aggressive outreach strategies, including the offer of translating and interpreting services; transport where necessary; and efforts to build the confidence of parents and model the respect in which they are held. Showing respect for families is achieved in several ways. One important factor is to take seriously service accessibility, be it geographical, access criteria or opening hours. Another key factor is to employ staff who are willing and responsive to parents.

There are special considerations which need to taken into account when planning the delivery of services within rural areas. These can range from the use of a mobile bus, incorporating play and advice facilities, to the maximizing of the use of premises belonging to universal services, such as schools and GP surgeries. There is also a place for linking the location of family centres to existing community centres.

The experience of family centres suggests strongly that families need a broad range of interventions which include both practical services and more complex work, such as enhancing parenting skills. Children's centres need to be engaged in both early intervention work and also work with those families who present more immediate child protection concerns to agencies. In spite of different referral routes and levels of professional concern about their parenting capacity, in reality, the services which will make a difference to achieving positive family outcomes are remarkably similar.

Chapter 6

Centres as a Gateway to Other Services

The Experience of Family Centres

A major part of this study has been concerned with the role of family centres in acting as a gateway to other services. The function of acting as a gateway to services will inevitably comprise a central role in the new arrangements currently being made by children's services authorities. Much can be learned from this study about the co-ordination and facilitation of integrated services.

The findings from the study showed that over the preceding decade some family centres, in particular local authority units, had developed from providing nursery services, which were almost exclusively child care facilities, to providing wide-ranging family support services. Although sometimes having strong initial reservations, family centre workers had been trained and developed to make the transition from a child care to a family support role, and so were well placed to appraise their capacity and potential to act as a gateway to other services.

Co-ordinating services for families

Some family centres in the review survey saw a main part of the gateway function as enhancing the co-ordination of local services. This process could be seen from either side of the gateway. First, centres acted as a gateway for families to access other services, which could be alternative, supplementary, or subsequent to those on offer in the family centre. A second aspect of co ordination was the provision of a gateway for professionals in other agencies to access families using the family centres who might need the service of other agencies.

Family centres reported they were co-ordinating their activities with a wide range of external services and other agencies. These included: health, education, mental health, pre-school advisory services, midwives, Homestart, local voluntary organizations, and housing departments. According to findings from the review survey, assessment, collaboration and a collective approach to services were essential key aspects of the process if it was to have positive outcomes for all the stakeholders involved. One centre manager said:

> We identify services related to need, arrange visits, co-ordinate staff work, liaise with other agencies and partners to ensure children and families receive appropriate services.

Barriers and boundaries to a co-ordinating role

There were factors which could constitute barriers or impose boundaries on successfully undertaking a co-ordinating role. Such impediments were cited by 17 per cent of family centres in the review survey. The main barriers to the development of a co-ordinating role for the family centre tended to be organizational ones:

> Co-ordination is usually done by social workers or the access team. We do recommend other services but cannot commission. Co-ordination would involve a change of policy and additional staff. This would require 'joined-up thinking' by the borough and a clear 'pathway' identified by a family support strategy, with a clear role identified for our family centre as the co-ordinator for early years provision; our local authority is not very good at that.

Taking a co-ordinating role was identified as requiring a clarification of roles and the reaching of agreements between agencies. It was also seen as often requiring extra staff to undertake the necessary work. Some family centres in the survey had recently taken over case management responsibilities. This development was associated with an increase in liaison with other agencies, an increase in late intervention work, and a decrease in early intervention work, with related changes in accessibility:

> After referral, other needs may emerge that we could help with. When we review our work we may decide with the client that other services should be offered.

> We do not as yet have caseholding responsibility but we do play a role in the co-ordination, identification of services to meet the needs of the child and family.

It appeared that the range and nature of staff qualifications in the family centres were critical factors in determining whether or not caseholding responsibilities were devolved to family centres:

> We don't have a qualified social worker in the centre to undertake initial assessments, so we could take the wrong route. Therefore we don't have a caseholding role for the main part.

To date, we have not been asked to undertake a caseholding role. We have staffing difficulties and training issues that prevent us from carrying out this work.

A collective approach to service provision

In spite of these constraints, there was evidence that family centres and other agencies adopted a range of approaches to the task of working together in order to co-ordinate and provide family support services. These included:

- Provision of commissioned/collaborative services: this involved providing services on behalf of another agency.

- Provision of collaborative services: this might also include purposive mixing of family centre staff with professionals from other agencies to provide a specific service in order to run a group, with shared input and responsibility.

- Provision of complementary services: family centres and other agencies might provide separate services to the same families to meet different needs. This could include commissioned working and family centres acting as a venue for other service providers to work with the family.

- Provision of an integrated service: this would mean family centres and other agencies had an explicit joint plan of work for the provision of family support services where they could call on each other to provide their respective inputs to the family.

These different aspects of working together are explored in the following section.

Commissioned services

Commissioned services were a feature of the majority of family centres. These commissioned services were of three types. Just under half of those commissioned were providing a mix of late intervention, early intervention and supportive services. Around one third were commissioned to provide early intervention services only and the rest were commissioned to provide late intervention services only (by social services). On top of these commissioned services, all the centres in the study were offering some services on their own behalf.

Collaborative services

Working together across agencies was a feature of many family centres, as suggested in Chapter 3. Our interviews with centre staff confirmed that there was active collaboration across a range of services, which spanned early and late interventions. It was noticeable that almost three fifths of centres were working with others in providing early preventive services. Just over one fifth collaborated on late or crisis interventions only and the rest ranged between planned and crisis work.

Complementary services

There were several ways in which family centres could complement the work of others. Family centres and other agencies frequently provided different components of the support services for the same family, and there was evidence to suggest that work undertaken by family centres in such situations was often carefully planned so as to 'dovetail' with other services. The following lengthy account, provided by a centre manager, demonstrates the considerable complexity of seeking to relate to a range of external agencies in the interests of providing a coherent service for families who have a range of needs:

> The school would refer to us regarding a particular difficulty and then we would undertake a review process. To put the work in progress, the school would be invited to that and would be part of it and we'd try and work in partnership with them so we're trying to think along the same lines. We would stay with the parents and they would try to do the same thing with the child.

> I suppose where health is concerned, lots of our referrals come from health visitors. And they're predominantly, obviously for under-fives. Looking at issues around behaviour management, health visitors are involved in our process in terms of doing initial visits, doing the review process, identifying who's doing which tasks.

> The families health visitors identify tend to be families who need longer, ongoing practical emotional support so they can go to other service providers and get the kind of individual type of therapy and those kind of things. But what they also need is the structures and routines and play work to be able to put some of that thinking into practice. And those aren't the bits that those other services, such as health or advice centres can always provide. So we would do lots about the children and go into the home and help families with those things. We'd provide ongoing support rather than individual sessions.

> Some centres work with the homeless but a lot of what they do is very practical stuff about benefits and housing and they run crèches and support groups and things like that. But when they identify issues to do with parenting then they refer the family to us and we'd work with them on that as well. So again we define roles so that families don't get the same things in two different buildings. So, in terms of our links and access that families can have, for example, if I've got a family with a fifteen-year-old that's having difficulty then I can go to the adolescent service and we can do joint pieces of work on that and so the family's familiar with us and familiar with the way we're working and so we can amalgamate reviews and between us we can joint work

things. If a family do a residential assessment and want to go back into the community, once their work finishes we come in and set about giving them general support.

Family centres complemented the work of other agencies by providing a connection between themselves and others in terms of space and place. They sometimes acted as a location for specific services provided by other agencies. For example, health visitors or community mental health teams could run independent groups on family centre premises for family centre service users and/or other families. Examples from the study included:

- regular parenting groups, looking at topics such as stages of development and children's behaviour

- one-off sessions such as 'establishing sleep patterns'

- support for special groups such as teenage parents

- post-natal depression groups

- mental health groups

- health promotion, such as smoking cessation, healthy eating, women and health

- drop-in advice surgery

- baby clinic facilities.

Using a family centre as a site for other services could also serve to make these services more acceptable and less stigmatizing to parents who might use them:

We run a group with mental health services here for mothers with mental health problems. There's a crèche provided so that's a support thing. It's supposed to take away some of the fear that often people with mental health problems have about us. It's about us trying to provide services in a non-stigmatizing way.

In addition, if other agencies came in and out of the family centre building, this could help to increase community awareness and acceptability of the family centre services. It also increased their acceptance as a complementary service. In this way it helped increase access:

There's a lot of things go on that we don't run now. WAVE [Women after a Violent Event], that's run by social workers and has been for a while now. The good thing for us about that is that people coming for that – and I think they've done other courses in the building – is that they might not have found their way here if they'd not come for WAVE. It just introduces them. We've had the technical college in to do lots of courses like some about self esteem, some about computers and we've done a crèche for them. We help those wanting to return to work as well as those with English as a second language.

So that's us making use of the building and trying to use the building to attract other people's expertise and knowledge. Another thing we collected is a welfare rights service run from this building. Not by us, but we rent the room on a small rent to a service called WRAG [Welfare Rights Advice Group]. It started out life with advice to the Asian community and now it gives it to everybody. There must be more inter-agency and partnership work going on in this building than anything else.

An integrated service

The final role for centres as complementary services was that of sharing families. This was seen to lead to integrated working relationships, where two workers would be in touch with the same family to co-ordinate their activities and to ensure the family received the most appropriate services:

We do co-working and lots of liaison with the health visitors really. They really are our 'best friends' in some ways because we're working so closely along the same lines as they are really in terms of child development, support to families. They're very good at letting us know what's going on with families. It's them often following up non-attendance. If the family's not coming to the family centre, the health visitor will pop round and see what's happening. They'll come to the families' reviews. They'll follow up things that are happening here at home. It may be that the health visitor is doing some work at home where we're doing some work at the centre so there are several levels of co-working.

The role of centres as gateways to informal networking by parents

The preceding sections have explored the relatively formal collective service activity between agencies. There was also an important role for centres in facilitating informal links between service users. Family centres could provide a gateway to links with other families but this could sometimes be more complex than it might seem at the outset. We found that families attending family centres often had opportunities for developing social or support networks with other families. Family centre workers varied in their attitudes to the families' informal networking with each other, but overall were usually supportive of the process. However, in a minority of cases, there was evidence that family centre workers perceived networking between parents as potentially inappropriate or even dangerous, in that it could:

- act as a distraction from the formal, intensive work which represented the main purpose for attending
- lead to the development of cliques within family centres acting as a barrier to newcomers

- mix parents attending for reasons of child abuse with vulnerable families, in conditions of confidentiality
- mix parents with similar problems which could in certain circumstances reinforce undesirable behaviours and/or beliefs
- pressure families into a social situation against their better judgement.

The views of family centre workers serve to illustrate the complexities of developing informal networks. Sometimes informal networking was encouraged:

> To help us with our days out for the families, we've tried to encourage that more because we'll say to someone, 'We can't manage all these children' and you see another mum who's got five kids on her own, then we'd ask somebody else to help her out as well. So, yes, we do and we've seen natural links start.

However, such social situations could be unpredictable and difficult to monitor and manage:

> When we go on the family day out, they are exhausting. It sounds like a nice thing to go for a picnic but it is a very hard thing for the staff to undertake because you are watching and you are working the situations all the time. No one should get isolated from the group and feel they've got to sit away from them with their children. Equally, somebody who's getting very irate with their children might end up being isolated by the other parents so all the time you're having to help the families to make sure that things are carrying on.

There were also perceived disadvantages in linking up parents with similar serious problems:

> There's a lot of pluses but not all situations are positive. If you've got somebody who has a drug issue, and they're coming to us for work with parenting, while they're coming off the drugs, they might well be in a group where there is somebody else who is also using. Then you've got to weigh up the pros and cons of, 'What are we doing here? Is it right?' and it is very dangerous. So sometimes you couldn't offer one service if it's going to be more dangerous to that person. So it's always a case of making sure you've got your head together when you're trying to put families together and you must not make any assumptions that it is going to be a good idea.

> We have a lot of women who come with depression and the positive is it's good for people with depression to know other people are the same, but sometimes a depressed woman doesn't want to sit with another depressed woman – so it is quite complex.

> If a lot of the people who come here are isolated and in some ways vulnerable and inadequate, what you don't want to do is form a group of people that are vulnerable and inadequate.

It was even felt that parents and children could be at actual risk from increased contact with other parents where there were serious safeguarding concerns:

> We've had one or two difficulties at some point. Sometimes the parents are very needy parents themselves and can often latch on to somebody who's quite vulnerable and we always have workers working in the social group. Because you've got people coming here who have abused children and you've got to be so aware – they've got a Schedule One offender that's coming in and you've got all these vulnerable families and children around. We've got to make sure that we know the person and that somebody's going to be around. You could be putting other families at risk.

Networking was not seen as solely the domain of adults but could involve children too. Usually this occurred in centres where there were children of school age. In most of these cases where this happened, the work of using groups to increase children's confidence and self esteem was seen as a signifi-cant part of the work of the centre:

> We're working with children to help them improve their social skills. We make contact with them early on to help them interact with their peers and talk to other children. We build their confidence up. And many of them they're at the beginning where perhaps families have separated out and they're feeling they're the only children whose mum and dad don't live together so they're in a group where other children are experiencing the same thing so their networks start. They're networking too. And we move them on when they're at a stage where the group is functioning beautifully, and they're coming in and there aren't any issues. They need to move on and we would help the parents to look at Scouts, Beavers, Cubs, Rainbow Club so the children can continue to expand their networks and have opportunities to be with other children.

Collating and disseminating information

Collating and disseminating information was another important role for family centres. Whether or not centres facilitated the sorts of service access and networks we have been describing was likely to depend, in no small part, on the information that parents in the community can access about services. We now turn to the role of centres as the collators and disseminators of information.

In order to link families to services, family centres frequently acted to collate and disseminate information about services. Using data from family centres and from parents, the study looked at the content, form and purpose of such information-giving.

Family centres frequently displayed a multi-faceted approach to informa-tion-giving, in terms of general and specialized information and advice, passed on through discussion, leaflets, reference materials, speakers, and by staff training and the involvement of informed parents:

> So we're known as an information and advice centre as well as a family centre. The information and advice side is very much benefits led – it's about benefits, housing. We've been able to get people into accommodation quicker than they can themselves because we know the information and can shortcut. We can name Section 17. We can quote the Children Act to housing and we get people in quicker. Well, we have all the different kinds of information about benefits and all the kind of forms we need to give people, such as housing benefit and disability forms. We also leave around leaflets for people to read for themselves. Besides this, a lot of the staff who work down here would know about those things and would be able to go through the form with the client. We also get people in, like the lone parent advisers who can advise about going back to work and the linked benefits. We get organizations in to give talks about changes in the benefits and we would go to these too to keep up to date. But then we also have people like the Body Shop coming in and giving talks about make-up, so we're making it as varied as we can. What we do is leave the information there to be available for parents or encourage other mums to speak to somebody who has been in the same situation because they've been through the same situation much more than I have. I don't know what it's like to live with violence. I don't know what it's like to not have enough money. I haven't experienced that but they've experienced that themselves.

Through this combination of written information and spoken explanation and advice, family centres aimed to reach families with varying language and literacy abilities. For example, written information was frequently available in a number of languages and multi-lingual staff and interpreters were often on hand. Overwhelmingly, literacy or understanding of English were not automatically assumed:

> All our materials are translated. Our information booklet goes out to parents, and we've actually had this put on tape this time in different languages, because we felt it was more user-friendly.

In family centres we visited, the presentation of written information varied from essentially 'scruffy' to essentially 'glossy'. It included folded photocopies, glossy brochures, leaflets stuck to walls, leaflet racks, and information reference libraries. Access to information was sometimes directly accessible and sometimes accessible to parents via family centre workers.

Furthermore, some family centres specialized in providing information and advice, such as helping families to manage social security benefits and housing problems more rapidly and effectively. Otherwise, if they did not have this expertise, they could mediate information from appropriate external information sources.

Barriers to the provision of information

In spite of family centres being able to facilitate access to other services and to information, this was not entirely straightforward. There could be barriers. Where there were pressures to narrow the family centre role and reduce the range of services, information collection and dissemination activities within family centres could be curtailed, as this example shows:

> The risk is that if we stop engaging so much with the community, new staff will get to a point where they don't see us doing that hour, sitting down with a woman and saying 'What does your child need?' Parents ask advice like, 'Is a child minder better than day care – which is best?' Some parents go to work but don't know about Family Credit and about tax. We've got a tick list – like a referral form. We've got a whole list of under-fives centres; a whole list of adult education and a whole list of play groups where you have to stay with them. Every week there is something new and, the moment I hear about it, I put it on my list. The under-eights information is in the central library – I'm going to find out where the adult stuff is – I'll have to put them on a sheet and then hand out bits of paper rather than do the hour. It's a shame because that hour is an important emotional thing.

Although some family centres, who had a restricted role, provided information on alternative and supplementary sources of support, others provided only limited information or, in some cases, no information at all:

> The only place that we do provide information is in our waiting room and we actually do have that on the wall and on the table and in the bookcase there. It is available but it's not developed. I actually think it would probably need a sort of strategy to really develop it more.

Parents' perspectives on the availability of information

Alongside the views of the centres, we thought it important to get parents' perspectives on their family centres' information-giving role. Eighty-three parents were interviewed across 28 family centres (see Appendix).

Tables 6.1 and 6.2 show that the majority had received information, and that very few had not received information that they wanted. Information was more likely to be offered rather than needing to be requested by parents and to be spoken than written or a combination of both.

Parents' access to information

Ninety-six per cent of parents in the study felt that there was someone at their family centre that they could approach for information and 84 per cent felt that there was more than one person that they could ask. Their comments strongly indicated that they found staff helpful, willing, approachable and easy to talk to:

I can talk to all of them at drop in and have a 'phone number at home so I can ring them up; staff ring and tell me about anything that might be interesting for me or the children to come to – activities, events.

However, where only one member of staff acted as a source of information, there could be problems:

It's confusing – the key worker left and there's workers leaving all the time so there's nobody specific to ask and no meeting of new workers so I don't know who to talk to now – it could be more organized here.

Some parents were reluctant to share information with new workers with whom they had yet to build trusting relationships:

My key worker has just left and so there's no one to approach now; I wouldn't be happy talking to staff now – I trusted my key worker and she's now left.

Table 6.1 Information format for parents

Information format	Percentage of parents
Spoken	33
Spoken and written	25
Written	21
No information	21

n=83

Table 6.2 Information delivery to parents

Information delivery	Percentage of parents
Offered/supplied	58
Requested/supplied	38
Offered/refused	3
Requested/not supplied	1

n=83

In summary, parents referred to a wide range of information and advice made available to them about other people or agencies who might be able to help, including:

- welfare rights and benefits advice, including information on Disability Living Allowance, DSS/Social Fund, Family Tax claims

- health advice on special conditions and on child development, available regularly from health visitors at the family centre

- housing advice: housing benefits; a housing action group

- advice on legal issues, including immigration

- advice on school issues.

What lessons can the experience of family centres contribute to the co-ordination of children's services?

We found that family centres played an important role in multi-agency working by linking families with other agencies. They did this in a variety of ways, some of which were misleadingly simple. For example, the provision of information was sometimes a key component of linking families into other networks. Should a parent approach a family centre worker with a request for information about language needs, for example, an experienced worker could use this interchange to explore any other needs which the parent might have but be reluctant to articulate. Domestic violence and substance abuse problems were good examples of such potentially sensitive and stigmatizing areas.

Children's centres will be sited in the same geographical areas as family centres and will be seeking to offer a service to many of the same families who currently access and use the services of family centres. Therefore, children's centres should not under-estimate the value of providing 'a subtle approach to signposting'. A request for information on one topic can, of itself, provide an opening to offer families further services. In other words, centres need to be open to opportunities to co-ordinate a range of services that may be provided in house or in partnership with a range of others.

We concluded that the giving of information needs to be a central feature in the work of the centres. At the same time, strategies need to be in place to ensure the continuity of knowledge. Where specialist information is in the hands of a few, it should be recognized that there can be problems if personnel leave, and knowledge and information can be lost. So, in order to be able to disseminate information when it is needed, the more mundane, back-room tasks, such as keeping information up to date, also need attention. The provision of information, while a key component of linking families into other networks, also provides an opportunity to stay in touch with other agencies. Centres need to establish systematic procedures for informing each other of new services coming on stream. In other words, the tasks of information seeking and updating play a vital part in co-ordinating relationships between agencies.

Centre-based services clearly have the potential to enable families to help each other, as well as accessing services, and this can be very valuable. However, while creating links between families can be very positive, care needs to be taken in relation to any issues that might put children at risk of harm. Centre-based services can have the unintended consequence of encouraging links between the tiny minority of families whose children are at serious risk of a range of abuses. While centre policies should not be built around the dangers potentially imposed by a few, account needs to be taken of these hazards and the safeguarding of children should always be in mind.

Chapter 7

The Importance of Centre Managers and Staff

In any agency, the staff and managers have a major impact on the outcomes for children and families who use the service. The *Every Child Matters* agenda emphasizes the importance of developing the children's services and social care workforce. This process is heavily dependent on the creation of more and better training arrangements and opportunities. For social care, the following four specific objectives have been identified.

- Improve supply and stability, through effective recruitment and retention.
- Improve quality through training and development.
- Promote innovative ways of working within social care and between it and other sectors.
- Promote stronger leadership, management and supervision, underpinned by the effective dissemination and embedding of good practice so that children and young people's needs and wishes are heard and influence those responsible for their safety and protection. (Department for Education and Skills 2004a, p.42).

The value of these objectives was borne out by our findings in relation to the nature and quality of the work undertaken by staff in family centres. This was closely associated with the attributes and abilities of family centre workers themselves. In this chapter, we explore a range of topics relating to the quality of the workforce, including staffing structures, staffing patterns and staff development, as well as training.

Staff teams

As suggested earlier, family centres have had a dynamic history, having in many cases evolved from existing projects, such as day nurseries. This evolutionary development has often had implications for the identity and skill mix of the respective staff groups already in place. Given that many modern family centres will have developed from day nurseries, this has frequently initiated a process of staff development and expansion. This process is often still ongoing, as family centre workers and their managers continue to develop their respective roles to meet changing needs and new policy agendas. Staff teams in the study represented the origins of the service. They were likely to include, to a greater or lesser degree, workers qualified in child care – Nursery Nursing Education Board qualifications or National Vocational Qualifications. These qualifications were likely to be supplemented by additional training and further qualifications.

The study found that staff teams varied considerably in terms of:

- size of staff group

- employment status i.e. paid or volunteer

- allocation of roles

- ratio of workers to families

- gender

- ethnicity

- degree of multi-disciplinarity.

How the staff groups looked

We found a variety of models of staff teams in the centres we studied. For example, in the intensive sample, staff teams had an average of seven workers, with the largest team having 29 paid staff. At the other end of the range, the smallest team in an independent family centre combined a small number of paid workers with volunteer support. The following example shows the demands on centres which had a small staff complement, resulting in the need for one person to take on a variety of roles simultaneously:

> The staff team is me! With no formal training whatsoever for this role, there's always help at the end of the 'phone. There are lots of support services in the area for voluntary groups and for development workers. There is funding advice, management advice – all aspects. I work 20 hours a week – my title is project worker – but I'm more of a project manager now. It takes me away from hands-on work with the groups – which I don't like. But if I wasn't doing what I was doing, there wouldn't be any groups. We have an admin person who does six hours a week although she does it on a fortnightly basis. She does two full days a fortnight. There's now the under-fives worker for 20 hours a week and the other employee is our cleaner who is also one of our staunchest volunteers as well for the groups. I'm a volunteer as well. A lot of

my after-school stuff is voluntary at the moment. And the time I spend in schools is extra to the time I spend here as well. So I'm probably full-time. But I believe in the project as you've probably gathered from how I've been talking about it. And I think it's that enthusiasm that comes across and wins over families.

We found a wide range of work roles within family centres, and core roles included:

- managers and deputy managers
- administrative staff
- domestic support and caretakers
- contact supervisors
- paid and voluntary counsellors
- crèche organisers
- family workers, family centre workers, family support workers
- nursery officers
- play workers
- project workers
- senior practitioners
- sessional workers
- specialist workers, including social workers.

Core roles could be supplemented by specialist input from practitioners from other agencies, such as speech and language therapists, health visitors and psychologists, based within family centres on a full or part-time basis.

Managers reported that they could expand their staffing and provision of administrative support, counselling and various group activities by offering a range of work experience placements:

And I have a very good developing relationship with the local further education college. They provide child care students who come on placements here. They're now providing for our admin. We have students for special needs theory and we even get students who are doing aromatherapy and hairdressing, things like that. They're actually quite useful. Although they have needs as well they certainly boost the variety of things that we can offer.

We have people from the community who need experience to use the photocopier, whatever. They would come for four weeks placement. They wouldn't access confidential information but they would be in the drop in and they would be making tea, they would be answering the 'phone ... for them to go back to employment. Sometimes, it's actually hard – they want to stay here and we have to say goodbye to them because we need to give the place to somebody else.

Staff teams had varying proportions of full-time, part-time and sessional workers as well as volunteers and parent helpers:

I have a staff team of ten. I'm the manager. I've got two senior support workers. That means there must be seven family support workers. People always say to me, 'You've got a big staff team' but we haven't because I'm covering the district.

We're actually quite a small team in our centre. There's myself and Anne, who are full-time. Anne is the deputy. And we're both social work qualified. All of the rest of the team are part-time so we've got one social work post which we've just recruited to so we've got a vacancy at the moment, that's 20 hours. We've got two family centre worker posts that are 30 hours a week and one family centre worker post that's 15 hours.

The ratio of staff to families also varied considerably. The numbers of families could be expressed as 'families on the books' or 'individuals seen per week'. One centre explained that, at any one time, they were likely to be working with about 80 families. Their staff group comprised eight full-time equivalents but, in reality, consisted of 14 individuals. This number included full-time and part-time family centre workers with social care qualifications and full-time qualified social workers and part-time senior social workers. Inevitably, the management and staff development tasks involved in looking after such a complex group were demanding.

Gender

We found low levels of male workers across all the family centres in the study. Indeed, for gender, the imbalance was likely to be considerably greater than that for ethnicity:

And we've got quite a diverse staff team – mainly women – we only have one male member of staff. But in terms of ethnicity it's quite broad.

Men were rarely employed in the family centres in the study. Of our intensive sample, 11 per cent of centres employed male as well as female staff and 15 per cent employed male managers. Varying degrees of concern were expressed by female staff about the disparity but for the most part, the value of having staff of both genders was increasingly being recognized:

We've never had that as an issue so we never think about it. We don't have men staff here – all the staff are women. Not deliberate, it's just the type of work that we do. It's mostly grass roots work in social work they're all women and then managers are male. But we do have at the moment two students who are male and it's very interesting having men as workers in the centre. It's a different, positive model for some children. Ideally I'd love a man here full-time because I think that kind of image – a positive male role model – is important for the children and for the women.

Some centres felt there was a major role for male workers in all mainstream children's services, including family centres. One positive input in centres would be their ability to counteract children's previously negative experience of men:

> We have over the years had more male nursery officers and I've worked with them and the positive impact of that, especially where you've got children where the man has been an offender in some way. Where there's been domestic violence. Actually being able to see men in a different role I think is really important to young children because they're forming their values about things and I think that they pick up their messages and all that sort of stuff at that very early age and so that's important for them.

Although there was a general view that more men should be employed in family centre work, this tended to be envisaged in terms of specialist work with fathers rather than as general involvement in the work of the team. In other words, male workers were seen as being useful for increasing the range of services for special groups rather than making an equal and substantial contribution to the mainstream services.

Family centres who were keen to employ more male workers saw this as a way to increase the engagement with the centre of fathers in the community, as well as bringing a different approach to family centre work. The need for an appropriate approach to engage fathers has been noted by other research (Ghate *et al.* 2000). Managers discussed the advantages, particularly for fathers and older boys, in terms of the accessibility and acceptability of attending family centres:

> If you have a significant number of male staff that makes it more comfortable for men to feel that they can come in. Men have some quite good ideas as well. Bob is forever finding new ways of trying to engage the men, make them feel it's worthwhile. His latest scheme was to use some of the garden and do some gardening and then get the men working on something which gave them some sense of fulfillment while they were doing the other bits of work as well. So he's developing that way and trying it out really to see what happens.

Black and ethnic minority workers

The issues of engaging black and minority ethnic families in family centres have been studied by Butt and Box (1998). In our study, the presence of black and minority ethnic staff had a considerable impact on the work of the centre. Where we found few or no black and minority ethnic workers, culturally specific services were less likely to be routinely provided. There was a widespread view that such services could only be adequately provided through the involvement of black and ethnic minority workers:

> We're an all-white staff so we feel we have nobody here who is qualified to do any identity work. We have once or twice used consultants for specific issues or we can borrow people from elsewhere.

Where we found a multi-cultural or multi-lingual workforce, there was much greater evidence of culturally specific services being provided. For example, a voluntary sector family centre manager had been asked by social services to develop a service in response to the needs of accommodated children with dual heritage:

> Look, we've got quite a few children in the care system who are of mixed parentage, who are with white carers, who are losing their sense of identity. We were asked, 'Can you do something?' So we said, 'OK, but you need to give us time to research it and we'll put a programme together'. So we did that and put a programme together on working with groups of children from the care system. We're now moving on to do it with individuals. And I've got staff who can speak all the Asian languages, so we're aiming to be in a position to work with any combination of ethnicity and culture.

The issue of language was an important one. The study found that family centres preferred to use their own multi-lingual staff rather than interpreters, in order to facilitate direct communication between staff and parents:

> We realized early on that if you want the Asian community in then you've got to have an Asian person to represent them, to be able to speak their language – you can't do it just through interpreters. So I got a Bengali worker, Gujarati, Punjabi and between them they can speak Urdu and many other languages. So we can cover all the Asian languages. And we used to have two African Caribbean workers but unfortunately as things have gone the workers have left and we've not been able to replace them. So that's what we're basically short of – an African Caribbean worker. But there is a centre in the next estate for the African Caribbean community.

The study found that, where there were low numbers of multi-lingual staff, there was usually no option but to employ interpreters, who might 'embellish' interpretations and sometimes constitute a potential barrier between parents and workers, especially if they were family members. Some centres were struggling with working across different cultures:

> And there are only two black members of staff this side in the family centre. Although we are in an Asian community, we've got two language speakers if we're lucky and the interpreter because he's a bit set in his views, I'm saying to him, 'I want you to do this for me, don't interpret just say exactly and tell me

exactly – don't change it, don't add anything'. We get situations where the husband will talk to the interpreter afterwards and then he'll say, 'No, no, she doesn't need that. She'll be OK. She'll do that on her own'. It really is hard. We're using people from her culture, but it just doesn't work on our terms sometimes if we are trying to reach the women's needs as we see them.

Resources for staff development

Access to continuing professional development was a major issue for all staff, irrespective of background. We looked at both the availability of opportunities to develop experience in providing new and/or specialized services and actual access to training.

We found that local authority staff were, on occasion, moved between family centres, both as an aspect of their own personal professional development and in order to support the development of specific family centres:

> What we're doing each time is co-opting a member of staff from another family centre. This person has run the positive parenting course three times so that eventually all of our staff will have an opportunity to learn how to do it.

> Our plan had been with all of our new groups where we didn't have people who were experienced in running the type of group, we would basically contract someone to come in and then one of our workers would work alongside them to learn the skills of running that particular group. They'd run two or three times and then our worker would actually take it over.

Where the family centre was developing its role and range of services, there was scope for family centre workers to increase their formal qualifications. There was an increasingly perceived tension between workers who were seen to know about child development, on the one hand, and those who were seen as doing something called 'social work', on the other. As suggested in earlier chapters, the latter was often narrowly perceived as the use of authority within child protection statutory powers:

> You need the balance. You need someone who's got the nursery nurse background and a social work qualification too. Or you need a team that's got some of both.

This manager reminded us that the Children Act 1989 placed child development at the centre of services for children in need (Department of Health 1990). She was striving to provide a programme of training opportunities which would enable the staff in her centre to supplement their existing professional knowledge so they would have a more informed view of each other's roles and responsibilities. She was very concerned about the tendency of previous nursery staff to see social workers as child protection investigation workers who merely 'enforced the law'. Another manager stressed the importance of developing a 'common ground' on which social workers and other staff could develop their services.

Family centres in the study varied in their access to training opportunities. For example, local authorities were not consistent as to the extent of training available, some limiting training to staff in their own family centres, while others accepted staff from independent/voluntary sector family centres too.

Some independent and voluntary sector family centres were in a position to train and develop staff, while others could provide very little training, and this was likely to be limited to training around specific policy-related issues. Sometimes they could access free training from other sources, such as that provided by their local social services, or training paid for by staff themselves:

> A lot of the training that we go on is either local authority training or could be other training that other organizations would put on. We have a fairly small budget for training – getting smaller and smaller each year. Because we are a voluntary organization, everything we get is put back into the organization. We don't have the million pound budget that social services have so, if it's training for us, it has to be appropriate training, not just training for the sake of training.

Training, whether centrally provided or run by family centres themselves, included:

- basic training such as child protection issues

- training and support for organizational responses to government initiatives coming on stream, such as Quality Protects

- rolling programmes of training around child protection and family support

- training on subjects such as stopping smoking and healthy eating, often provided by invited trainers and speakers.

Interviews with staff indicated that some of them were sometimes reluctant to participate in new training and styles of work, but they were expected to attend:

> Some staff are change-weary, there's no doubt about that. Some staff have been around a long time and just wanted to do child care and didn't necessarily want to do family support work particularly, you know, so there's a mix here. It would be naïve of me to say everyone's happy with everything that's going on. Some would rather be writing up their notes but every member of staff is part of a development group on the subject or issue that they are interested in. So the groups look at issues of encouraging more male carers and delivering services for black and ethnic minority families and quality in play services for children with a disability. There is that choice. They all go into groups and produce action plans and things we want to do. So we're carrying

that on now. And we meet as a whole service every other month and we do some sort of presentation and group exercise and that's to get people mixing.

Restrictive pressures on staff development

In addition to the obvious direct effect of financial constraints, there were also indirect financial and policy pressures affecting staff development. While some family centres were working to extend their range of services and individual staff, others were subject to pressures to reduce services and staff or to reduce staff teams. This had resulted in alterations, and often reductions, in services.

The long-standing national crisis in social work recruitment and retention sometimes meant that family centre workers were expected to make good the shortfall in the local authority. While the staff we interviewed were supportive of individual opportunities for career development, concern was expressed that such enforced moves might aggravate tensions between social work teams and family centres:

> Our nursery officers will be called something else. They'll be called 'family support workers' or 'unqualified support workers' or 'a shoulder to cry on'. And there's a fear in that for me because social workers have always been the ones with a little bit more power, a little bit more clout.

Family centre staff were concerned that nobody would be trained as a nursery officer in their own right. One manager was particularly worried that the skills of nursery workers would be overtaken by a preoccupation with other tasks, such as project management. At the same time, this manager also recognized that her staff were favourably placed with regard to training, compared with social workers:

> The poor old social workers, because they're all sick and covering each other's jobs they don't get any training.

Conversely, another manager, used to employing some social workers, was very worried that preventive work was increasingly excluded from the social work role and was being given to other staff, who may or may not be appropriate to carry out the work. This had important implications for the roles and tasks of trained social workers and the impact on services offered to children in need and their families:

> Because they've got such a problem, they're drafting the nursery officers in as 'unqualified welfare workers'. The department is calling them 'unqualified social work people' and, of course as managers, we have the opposite problem. We keep saying, they may be qualified for us. It's just that they are not qualified with a social work qualification.

Although this could present opportunities for social care staff, it might also place such staff inappropriately into roles such as specialist court and adoption work, with the result that they would defect from family centres to other family support roles, which promised a circumscribed remit of family support work:

> There's a positive move for a lot of staff but I think several are thinking they don't want to end up giving evidence in court cases – they're not paid enough. They'll go to Sure Start or they'll go to Education or they'll go to – well, all the little nurseries springing up with the IT centres, in fact, the private ones.

How do workers support each other?

There was no doubt that, in spite of good management in many cases and a supportive environment, family centre work was seen as being stressful and, consequently, required a high level of mutual understanding and support between workers:

> Certainly for the staff who are working closely with families, tremendous stress and strain, there really is a huge amount and that's one of the reasons that we don't have a big turnover but we do accept that staff will leave.

One manager explained that her family centre had a policy to try to identify stress early on so it could be dealt with. Where staff were absent for three occasions, she would interview them in a supportive way to try to explore their situation and find out whether the absence was caused by stress. She was aware that staff could become completely absorbed in their work and 'not be able to switch off'.

In another centre, the manager stressed the use of the weekly staff meeting as one means of managing stress:

> The first hour of the staff meeting is a support thing because it is extremely stressful and dangerous at times from the point of view of the child because there are the occasions where the families come in because of concerns over such and such and it can still be carrying on.

This manager was very aware of the way in which the team meeting could be used to share knowledge and experience across the staff group:

> One of the things that I actively encourage is people's gut feelings. It might not be worth much in court but you can warn other people. They'll say things like, 'There's something going on. I don't know what it is but ...' I always say, 'Share it with your colleagues so we can keep an eye on it'. And that's one of the things we're going to get across to new staff is that the unbelievable actually is believable and it does happen. Things they've maybe never even thought about – don't be surprised.

To counteract stress, attempts were made to rotate the degree of stress under which staff worked:

> Not one worker does all the assessment and that's because it's very shattering. We look at it like a cycle: they go around and they can do all the practical bits. They've got all their sessions worked out; they do all the bits to it and then they get a fortnight or ten days writing up. This is inbuilt.

This manager took her responsibilities for looking after the welfare of her staff very seriously:

> And we always watch staff who start to dip. So we go into supporting staff more or less according to need. Where you're rescuing staff, then you build them back up again so that they're able to take on the next assessment.

It was clear from the study that many family centres were trying hard to support and develop their staff. This chapter has provided a snapshot of the way family centres recognize and tackle these issues. The comments of managers and staff reflected the pressure under which staff work. At the same time, they revealed some of the strategies that good managers adopt to promote the welfare of their staff.

What lessons can family centres contribute to the development of the children's services workforce?

A major question must be addressed in taking forward the development of children's centres. What sort of career pathway will exist for staff in children's centres? Our findings showed that staff development played an important role in the ability of a centre to respond appropriately to the needs of families. The study underlined the value of having flexibility within one person's role across the workforce. For example, a staff member might be responding in the morning to the needs of a depressed mother, and in the afternoon, to the literacy needs of a child or parent.

Workforce issues within family centres are part of a wider crisis in the social work and social care workforce. As our study showed, short-term answers for some of the new agencies have involved poaching the staff of family centres. However, this strategy can, by definition, provide no long-term answer. Clearly, the way forward needs to involve a mix of methods around recruitment and retention. For example, the 'growing your own model' (Meadows and Garbers 2004), whereby mothers are encouraged to develop a range of skills and to pursue formal accreditation, may be one answer. In addressing these challenges, managers need to be sensitive to recruitment and retention trends in other parts of the workforce and to ensure that they play a leading role in the activities of the Children's Workforce Network.

The Children's Workforce Network (CWN) is a strategic body, bringing together the relevant Sector Skills Councils (including the Children's Workforce Development Council) and other partners. It is a voluntary grouping of independent partners, who recognize that collaboration will help them to achieve the more effective implementation of their individual and joint roles. The Network's vision is a children's workforce that:

- supports integrated and coherent services for children, young people and families
- remains stable and appropriately staffed, while exhibiting flexibility and responsiveness
- is trusted and accountable, and thereby valued
- demonstrates high skills, productivity and effectiveness
- exhibits strong leadership, management and supervision.

(Children's Workforce Network 2005)

Our study shows there is clearly a need for local strategic planning in relation to the workforce for children and families. Creative solutions to staff shortage might include the building of links with local colleges either as part of their training or as work experience. We endorse the view of the Children's Workforce Network:

The Children's Workforce Network believes the development of a coherent, skilled and effective children's workforce in England will be achieved through the development, monitoring, evaluation and review of a partnership-based multi-agency reform programme to:

- promote integrated ways of working
- create greater flexibility in career pathways
- bring about a positive culture change.

(Children's Workforce Network 2005)

We also found that there are considerable advantages to both staff and families if diversity of gender, race and ethnicity are represented on the staff group. Families can then have a choice over which staff members they relate to. Giving families choice is an important part of changing the culture in centre-based services to one which emphasizes the empowering of parents and sees them as experts on defining their own needs.

Our study resonates with the emphasis placed by the Children's Workforce Development Council (www.cwdcouncil.org.uk) on leadership. The best managers need to adopt strategies to prevent staff from becoming too stressed and can build in ways of working to protect staff from stress overload.

Finally, and perhaps most importantly, as our study shows, there can be considerable dangers for families and agencies in narrowing the roles of social workers to child abuse investigations. This hazard applies to a range of workers, including members of health and education agencies. Centre based services have an important two-way role to play in relation to the core curriculum for the child care workforce. On the one hand they can inform its design and, on the other, benefit from staff who have been the recipients of broad-based training in the developmental needs of children.

The significant workforce issues we found in the study are reflected in government's current objectives for the children's workforce. Indeed, our findings reinforce the views of the Children's Workforce Development Council. This body advocates priority should be given to networking to bring together the key partner organizations responsible for leading and influencing workforce development programmes for staff working with children and young people in education, health, play, social care, youth justice, and youth work. It recommends there should be:

1. Quality: work with partner organizations to ensure that members of the workforce have appropriate skills and knowledge to work together effectively to improve outcomes for children and young people.

2. Capacity: work with partner organizations to ensure the recruitment and retention of well-trained staff across all sectors of the children's workforce.

3. Pathways: work with partner organizations to improve access to flexible career pathways within and across sectors. Develop a more coherent career framework, incorporating common standards and qualifications wherever appropriate.

4. Cultural change: improve communication and promote buy-in within and across sectors to more effective inter-agency working and appropriate remodelling.

5. Network activity: oversee the implementation of a coherent programme for children's workforce reform. Influence the plans and activities of each individual member so that the developments in each sector are increasingly harmonized and mutually supportive.

6. UK: work within the framework of UK-wide Sector Skills Councils so that developments in England are harmonized as appropriate with other parts of the UK.

(Children's Workforce Development Council 2005)

Chapter 8

Parents' Perspectives on Family Centres

Current policy developments place a high premium on the engagement and ongoing involvement of parents in service design and delivery. Sure Start is probably the most high-profile example, so far, of an initiative which is based on a commitment to active parental engagement. Indeed, these developments echo the key principles of the Children Act 1989, which underline the importance of working in partnership with parents (Department of Health 2001). We were particularly concerned, therefore, to explore both the extent to which parents are involved in the operation of family centres, whether on a practical basis or in terms of decision-making, as well as their overall levels of satisfaction with the work of family centres.

Parental participation

We found evidence of significant participation on the part of parents in many of the activities of the family centre, such as child-related activities, including supervising and playing with children, help with stories, helping with refreshments, help with games and helping other parents when they needed a short break. There were also general activities such as making coffee, washing up, putting toys away and tidying up. Participation could be on a spontaneous basis:

> It depends a lot on what you want to do yourself – they don't force you to do things here.

It could also be organized on the basis of rotas within the framework of the more structured participation of volunteers or parent helpers:

> I take my turn every week to help tidy up and make the coffee.

Parents' views were invited on the level of opportunities overall for involvement in the operation of family centres, as well as their personal involvement. Table 8.1 shows that most of the parents interviewed thought that overall they had some degree of involvement, with just over half having the view that there was a high degree of involvement.

Table 8.1 Parental perceptions of levels of involvement

Level of involvement	Percentage of parents
High level	52
Low level	44
No involvement	4

n=83

In terms of their own personal involvement, 62 per cent of parents said that they were involved, either by committee membership, organizing groups and activities or contributing practical help. Although there were a small number of references to the active involvement of parents in the formal objectives of family centres, parents were more likely to refer to partnership in terms of involving individual parents in decisions about their own and their children's services.

Centre staff, both in the independent and the voluntary sector and also in social services family centres made reference to the following partnership activities:

- involvement of parents in annual service reviews

- encouragement of some parents to serve on management committees

- involvement of service users as fully as possible in the development and running of the service

- encouragement of centre users in the activities of the centre and its day-to-day management.

Some family centre managers, particularly in independent and voluntary sector family centres, described the involvement of parents in shaping the agency's policies:

> Our voluntary agency expects us to listen to the parents. That's very much part of the agency's philosophy. What the parents want, we're bound to provide. They're the ones that should have a say in what goes on. It's their family centre. We're just here to help them along the way. So when we took over, it was like ready to go as a really good parent-led family centre.

Parents' participation in decision-making

By contrast, in terms of decision-making, we found that parents were generally excluded from all but basic or superficial decisions. There were one or two exceptions, such as the centre that unusually involved families in decisions about staff appointments or which groups should be offered and who should run them. However, overall, levels of formal involvement in decision-making were dominated by more superficial day-to-day concerns such as whether to have fruit or biscuits for children's snacks; whether there should be smoking areas outside the building; what toys to buy; and choices relating to seasonal activities such as holidays and arrangements for the Christmas meal.

We found that there was a degree of competition for influence on decision-making in family centres. This was between funders (generally the dominant influence), managing organizations other than local authority social services, and family centre managers and workers. This rivalry served to put a 'squeeze' on the role and level of participation enjoyed by parents. Amid competing and more powerful influences, there was sometimes little scope for the involvement of parents in decision-making.

Some parents even commented that influence and participation were actively discouraged and clearly not wanted by family centres:

> They never seem to need us to help them decide things or even like us trying to do so. I think it's because of the mix of types of people, such as single mums, and poor families.

However, there were some indications that this situation could be changing.

> Decision-making – no, we are not involved but I think that is going to happen more as we are now allowed to go to the staff meetings.

> Staff want us to get more involved and we have agreed to it – the Centre is moving soon and we have to choose the furniture.

A small minority of parents were reluctant to participate in decision-making, not seeing it as part of their role:

> I wouldn't like to because I wouldn't like the responsibility.

> I'm not really keen on making decisions – my key worker is supposed to do that.

Parents' views on family centres

In addition to looking at the parameters of involvement and decision-making in family centres, we were very keen to obtain parents' overall views of family centre services. This was done by exploring levels of satisfaction with services provided by family centres.

We found that the parents participating in this study were more likely to be *unsatisfied* than *dissatisfied* with the service they received from family centres, in that they tended to want *more of the same* services rather than *different* services.

One way of looking at satisfaction is to assess how far expectations are fulfilled. Table 8.2 compares parents' reasons for attending family centres with their actual experience there. Overall, their positive experiences generally exceeded their expectations. There were some exceptions. These included the assessment of children's development, where parents had hoped to gain explicit explanations for their concerns about the lack of progress they thought their children were making. Another area that did not meet expectations was support for parents with mental health problems, who were dissatisfied with the intensity of support they received and would have valued more one-to-one intensive help. Some had expected more access to social activities. It could be that approaches to meeting such needs were not clearly recognized or defined, but staff expected, wrongly, that they would automatically meet in the course of general play activities, personal development opportunities and therapy services.

In interviews, parents were asked to say what they liked best about their family centres. Table 8.3 shows their responses.

The most frequently cited best aspects of family centres for parents was the atmosphere of the centre and the staff they encountered. This was an added value to the actual services and support received, but was nevertheless fundamental to parents' positive experience of family centres.

In family centres' aims and objectives, there were frequent references to creating a warm and welcoming atmosphere. As an indicator of the achievement of these aims and objectives, almost a quarter of parents in the study acknowledged that the pleasant atmosphere was for them the best aspect of their family centres. Comments referred to family centres as having an atmosphere that was good, friendly, lovely, relaxing or welcoming and being a home from home, a neutral place to meet, a place where children could be comfortable and safe, a place where parents did not feel they were under surveillance. They could ask for help without feeling they were being judged or put under pressure.

Parents appreciated their relationships with staff and interactions with other parents. Comments referred to staff as being: likeable, friendly, approachable, helpful, giving good advice, being good with the children and easy to talk to as well as knowing 'how to help mums'. Staff were generally perceived as being welcoming, friendly and open and parents appreciated feeling that everyone was treated the same.

Other best aspects of family centres cited by parents included easy access in a range of ways, such as being able to have a key worker, being able to join a support group, and being able to take part in a range of activities. These might include specific services for parents and children, such as learning how to play together and opportunities for personal and skill development at no financial cost to themselves.

Table 8.2 Reasons for coming to the family centre and what happened there

Activities		Percentage of parents	
		Reasons for attending	What happened
Child-centred	Child care/nursery/pre-school	16	27
	Child development assessment	19	5
	Play activities	16	78
	Support	25	35
	Social activities	61	48
Family-centred	Family activities	11	27
Parent-centred	Teaching parents to safeguard children (child protection work)	12	11
	Leisure activities	5	25
	Mental health support	22	11
	Parenting advice	28	49
	Respite care	13	13
	Social networks	48	40
	General support	34	69
	Personal development	0	51
	Facilities	0	12
	Therapy	0	6

n=83

Note: Responses on each dimension are more than 100 per cent in some cases as more than one response per parent was received

Less than half of parents could name an aspect of their family centre that they 'liked least'. Table 8.4 indicates that dissatisfaction was most likely to be related to the building and its location rather than the experience of family centre services. With the exception of the specific services mentioned above, such as the desire for more intensive one-to-one help, most of the negative aspects were

Table 8.3 The best aspects of family centres for parents

Aspect	Percentage of responses
Atmosphere	22
Staff	16
Support	14
Activities	12
Staff and service users	11
Everything!	10
Socializing	8
Facilities	5
Respite	2

n=83

Note. Responses on each dimension are more than 100 per cent in some cases as more than one response per parent was received

Table 8.4 The aspects of family centres least liked by parents

Aspect	Percentage of responses
Building	25
Funding	11
Facilities	8
Location	11
Not enough	14
Too general	14
Staff	7
No aspect like least	10

n=83 (otherwise nothing liked least)

more likely to be described in terms of not having enough of a particular service rather than the unacceptability of services received. There were a minority of parents who did not like individual members of staff. Sometimes this was a personality clash, but it could also refer to relationships where staff were challenging parents' attitudes.

For the majority of parents in the study, family centres represented the main or only source of family support. A minority of parents preferred the support provided by the family centre to that available to them within their own family networks. This was usually because they saw the offer of support from their family as undermining their confidence and abilities:

> My brother offers to help by taking the children off but I accept only occa-
> sionally. Unlike the family centre, he can't see that it's not a straight choice
> between the children being here at home and being with him. He means well
> but the family centre understands me better. I enjoy the children, they are my
> life. I don't know what to do when they are away. My brother doesn't under-
> stand this. He makes me feel stupid.

Parents' reactions to moving on

The underlying assumption of the majority of social care interventions for children and families is that the individuals concerned will experience some degree of progress, whether this is towards improved parenting, or enhanced outcomes for children, and, in the case of older children and young people, working towards an appropriate level of independence. This is as true of family centres as of other services for children and families. In some cases, the appropriate goal for a family will be to move on from a high level of support provided by the centre to a greater degree of independence. In other cases, families may need continuing and sustained support for several years. Given the adverse, complex situations, both personal and material, in which many of the families were living, their wish for access to the continuing services of family centres was really rather modest.

Unsurprisingly, the comments of parents in the study reflected this diver-sity of experience. Different individuals wanted different types and levels of services from the family centres to meet their own particular needs. These aspi-rations were reflected in their attitudes towards the centre when their contact with it was coming to an end.

We identified two broad models of service use, both of which had implica-tions for the task of 'moving on'. The first were where the use of the centre was *enduring*. In other words, some families were intensively involved with the family centre on a daily basis and because of their social and economic circum-stances, needed this level of support. These families were likely to be using family centres on an open-ended basis over potentially long periods of time:

> The centre is my life and my life is the centre.

A second group of families were using the centre on an *intermittent* basis. They had a different level of need and came to the family centre at times of crisis or when facing life transitions, for example, when another child was born:

> I like to know it's there though, if I'm honest, there will be whole periods when I don't need to pop in. But sometimes things change overnight. My eldest recently got arrested. I just needed to talk to someone and get some decent advice for me, as well as him. They were great.

Interviews with parents showed that they could be very appreciative of having access to family centre services and be reluctant to leave. They could be so reluctant to lose their eligibility for family centre attendance that they became distraught at the prospect, even considering further pregnancies in order to remain eligible:

> When my little one is old enough to go to school, my attendance stops. I ask myself, 'Do I get pregnant again so I can carry on attending?' I'd like to work here. There are so many deserving people, I feel privileged to come.

Other parents were mindful of, but resistant to, the possibility of becoming dependent:

> I depend on them – I need to move on and try not to use it too much.

However, one very positive outcome of the wish to remain connected to family centres was the transition some people made from using the service to becoming a helper, volunteer or community member:

> I'd be lost without it because it's like a meeting place for friends to get together – they have helped me and I like helping out – give some back.

What lessons can be learned from the experience of family centres about working with parents?

The reality for many families is that they do not have access to support for parenting within their own extended families, nor do they have easy access to support in their own communities. At the same time, it was clear from their views that they would value, were it available to them, the opportunity to draw on support from non-stigmatizing services within their local communities.

At the same time, the way in which such support is offered needs to recognize that parents are experts on their own strengths and needs. They themselves, if empowered to do so, can take an active and illuminating role in the assessment of their own circumstances. A parent-led approach to services needs to be built into service delivery, whether those services are open access with parents referring themselves or are triggered by referrals from professionals.

Services need to recognize that families themselves are diverse in a range of ways, including structure, ethnicity, special needs and material circumstances. At the same time, their needs are diverse in terms of length and intensity of service required from family centres. While many families will benefit from short periods of help and their children will demonstrate improved developmental outcomes as a result over a relatively short period of time, this will not be true for everybody. Other families will need help over several years. Even if they do not receive continuous support, they need to be able to return to the source of services, when they need help, over an extended period. Improved outcomes for their children will be dependent on access to services over the course of the childhood years.

Parents appreciate a range of services which are supportive both to them and their children. It is a mistake to under-estimate the extent to which the majority of parents aspire to be good parents. They generally want what is the best for their children. Parents who use family centres often want to use services in a way that will optimize the chances of their children having wider opportunities than they have enjoyed themselves.

What parents like about family centres is that the services are provided in the context of a warm and welcoming atmosphere. It was clear from parents' responses that the characteristics they associated with a positive atmosphere required both a lack of stigma and an explicit acknowledgement of their strengths by staff. Making a reality of this 'welcoming atmosphere' requires centre-based services to offer parents opportunities to meet and converse with other adults. Centres also need to offer parents the opportunity to develop their own personal and occupational skills, in addition to their skills as parents. Parents need centres to help them plan for their futures, not simply to address the deficits of their current parenting skills in the here and now.

Any service for parents with children of any age needs to aspire to providing an atmosphere that recognizes and affirms parental strengths. The new children's services agenda needs to take account of parents' views and offer them an inclusive role within centres. Only by empowering parents to reach their potential both in their parenting role and as adults, will children be the beneficiaries of supportive services. As John Bowlby, originator of attachment theory, said in the 1950s, 'if a society values its children, it must cherish their parents' (cited in Green 2003, p.5).

Chapter 9

Family Centres in Transition

There have been two over-arching and interlinked objectives to this study. Firstly, we set out to describe and explain the contribution which family centres have consistently made to the process of changing, for the better, the lives of children and families. Secondly, we wanted to identify their potential for continuing to do so in the future.

The study's findings painted a picture of ongoing changes in the way that family centres can, and do, operate. However, it is important to acknowledge that these pressures have both affected family centres and, simultaneously, have had a knock-on effect on the services which they have been able to offer families.

Change was a consistent feature of family centre work in the study. It derived predominantly from three sources. These were the pressures exerted by central government through new policy directions; the pressures from local government, through changing funding policies, including cuts in finance; and the changing priorities of partner agencies in both the voluntary and statutory sectors.

In this chapter, we present our findings under two main themes. The first theme is concerned with the overall picture of change. Secondly, we discuss possible explanations for the changing picture in respect of family centre work and service provision.

Overall view of changes in family centre work and service provision

At the review stage of the study, 344 family centres out of a possible 408, who were still in business, responded to us. Around three fifths of these family centres reported that they had experienced changes in services over the time of the study, 4 per cent of our sample having changed completely from undertaking family centre work to carrying out other functions. Fourteen per cent of our sample of family centres had experienced organizational restructuring, and a further 13 per cent were undergoing a service review at the time of the survey.

There was evidence that such reviews of service could be externally driven, for example as part of Best Value programmes, area-wide child care reviews, or internally driven, as a result of loss of funding.

The remaining two fifths of family centres said there had been no change. The reasons for this varied, and included:

- operating in conditions of stability and continuity in terms of needs, resources and influences

- not experiencing major changes in operation and accepting minor changes as implicit to family centre work

- being satisfied with the status quo and not wishing to respond to influences towards change

- being unable to respond to influences towards change

- being unwilling and unresponsive to influences towards change.

Changing trends

Table 9.1 and Table 9.2 present the trends in the changing patterns of main service provision. Table 9.1 shows changes in the category of late intervention services and Table 9.2 shows the changes in the category of early intervention services. Overall, 29 per cent of centres had experienced change in late intervention and 37 per cent change in respect of early intervention.

In general, across the two tables, increases in services were more likely to occur than decreases across statutory services, intensive services, such as child protection assessments, and community development/support services. There were also increases in services related to parenting behaviour. The pattern of change is complex.

Table 9.1 indicates that 8 per cent had seen an increase in their assessment work. There were also small increases in formal work such as supervising parental contact and working with families to restore children.

Findings from the review study indicated a trend towards higher thresholds, with an increase in reactive, crisis work, and an emphasis on the prevention of family breakdown. There were reports of increasingly complex work, in particular, assessments.

Table 9.2 shows that there were few changes to the scale of services generally associated with early intervention. The exception was a marked increase in respect of work targeted att changing the behaviour of parents, whther in a group setting (4%) or through one-too-one intervention (11%). There was a marginal increase in community development and support work and some increase in general group work.

Table 9.3 shows a small increase in services for children. There is, for example, an increase of support services for children, including out-of-school

Table 9.1 Late intervention service changes (review sample)

Service type	Percentage of family centres experiencing change (29%)	
	Increase	Decrease
Assessments	8	2
Contact	4	0
Court work	4	0
Crisis work	4	0
Restorative/rehabilitation work	3	0
Looked-after children	2	1
Adoption work	1	0

n=100 of the 344 in the review sample

Table 9.2 Early intervention service changes (review sample)

Service type	Percentage of family centres experiencing change (37%)	
	Increase	Decrease
Community development and support	5	4
Groupwork	6	1
Health project	1	0
Information service	1	0
Parent support groups	4	2
Parenting/family work	11	2

n=127 of the 344 in the review sample

activities. There was evidence of working with children with more complex needs and with primary school children with behaviour problems.

Table 9.3 Children's services changes

Service type	Percentage of family centres experiencing change (25%)	
	Increase	Decrease
Nursery education/early years/pre-school	3	2
Out-of-school activities	3	1
Day care	2	3
Play group	1	0
Children only work	5	2
Direct work with children	2	1

n=86 of the 344 in the review sample

It is difficult to draw very precise conclusions from such a complex pattern of change other than to suggest the following. First, that family centre services in the sample had increased in the diversity of their work. Second, that the increase had been in the context of services formally commissioned by the local authority which emphasized an 'immediate safeguarding' or child protection investigation approach rather than a 'promoting welfare' approach. This is also supported by a more interventionist approach to working with parents and children. Nevertheless, a sizeable proportion of family centres, during the course of the study, were able to maintain their current level of general support-ive services with continuing evidence of the use of groupwork.

There was some evidence of an increase in services with an educational bias, such as homework clubs and family learning; and for parents, information technology courses and programmes to help them prepare for returning to work were important. The requirements of referrers and funders were increas-ingly influencing specialization. For instance, a centre might be in the process of becoming an area assessment site or a multi-agency referral centre to social services for drug-misusing parents and their children. There were additional services for special groups, including support for pregnant and new mothers in general, and teenage mothers in particular; and parenting groups for step parents. There was also an increase in groupwork with families where there had been domestic violence.

Activities which focused on support for children took account of the needs of a diverse range of children. These included children with special needs, including young carers, looked-after children, children with disabilities and children of substance misusers. There were also reports of reductions in services for children with special needs to accommodate increases in other types of work, such as parenting assessments where there were care proceedings, and adult-focused groupwork on positive parenting.

Changes with regard to services for ethnic minority families were mentioned by only a minority of family centres experiencing change. Here, services were being developed as special projects, such as a race equality project funded by Single Regeneration Budget. There were also projects set up in response to local needs for specific communities and Yemeni and Turkish communities were two examples. Increasing efforts were being made to promote the inclusion of asylum seekers. One family centre reported the recruitment of an Urdu-speaking family centre worker to provide support for local families in their homes and to encourage them to access local provision.

Expansion of services included facilitation of links with the services provided by other professionals, for example, through sharing premises with child and adult mental health services, and child and adult psychologists and psychiatrists.

Changes in child care services were associated with increasing complexity, for example, in circumstances where day care would be provided only as part of an assessment package and would include both children and their parents. In some cases, these took the form of focused group care sessions incorporated into work plans for families. Other changes in day care included the replacement of an early years education nursery with a pre-school play group or full day care reduced to sessional care. There was also the discontinuation of in-house child care provision, sometimes replaced with bought-in services or sponsored private day care.

Changes in access and referral patterns

Alongside the changes in the pattern of services offered by family centres, we found evidence of changes in access and referral patterns. The two are inevitably interlinked, but it may be helpful to describe the detail separately. There was a wide range of reported changes in relation to service user access since the time of the earlier survey. Types of change were associated with children's age range, area and specialization.

Changes to referral procedures included the introduction of referrals instead of open access; restriction of referrals to health visitors and social workers; exclusion of self referrals; and the channelling and filtering of referrals through external assessment, which involved increasingly specific referral criteria. Conversely, referrals, particularly from education services, were increasing as a result of changes in funding.

Children's age and access

References to children's age represented 17 per cent of all specified changes relating to service users. There were examples of expansion from a focus on pre-school children to one that included primary school children. Some centres catered for most children, or all children and young people of school age. Specialized services increasingly targeted specific age groups, for example, the development of services for 5–13-year-olds who were affected by their parents' substance misuse. There was also an increase in working with older children with more complex needs. Workers indicated that they had seen a trend whereby more children in the 8–11 year age range, were referred because of behaviour in school or at home. In addition, there had been an increase in the number of core assessments requested by social workers for children under two years.

Area and access

Changes in the catchment area represented 8 per cent of all changes which were mentioned. Such changes included expansion of the area served, particularly to include rural areas; a compensation for inadequate or non-existent provision; or moving the site within a catchment area to increase accessibility and social inclusion.

Changes were also reported which related to a contraction of the area served. These changes were often associated with restrictions attached to funding from initiatives such as Sure Start, Single Regeneration Budget and New Deal for Communities. This focus on particular geographical areas was perceived by centre staff as having a constraining effect on who was eligible for what, perversely, could be substantially increased services:

> The majority of our services are now only for families who live in certain areas i.e. Sure Start and SRB areas – which actually overlap – so some people can have two bites of the cake whilst most people can have none.

Other issues arose when families were moved from their area as a result of housing projects or family centre buildings were demolished for private sector housing.

Changes of staffing in centres

Two important aspects of change revealed in the review survey concerned both the decrease and the increase in levels of staffing in centres. There was evidence of great effort being made to maintain services despite low levels of staffing:

> The balance of high to medium priority remains about the same. We are as creative as it is possible to be with a minimal staff of five, offering more programmes and innovative packages to meet individual need.

However, there were reports of groups being closed and of the introduction of waiting lists because of vacant posts. Some team members were seconded to Sure Start, developing valuable links with this initiative but leaving gaps in family centre provision. Family centres also reported a lack of volunteers and crèche workers, resulting in staff having to care for children while simultaneously running groups.

By contrast, there were also instances in which staffing had increased, as exemplified by one centre:

> The service is in a state of continuous evolution. The team has in the last five years grown from five at the inception to a projected 15 by next year.

However, even where staffing levels had been increased, there were suggestions that there were insufficient staff to cope with increasing workloads and responsibilities. The holding of more complex cases required the presence of staff qualified in social work, who were often not available. Outreach workers were recruited in line with the change to a mode of service delivery which emphasized home-based and community services. These would not necessarily involve changes to the content of services but would allow staff to engage with families in a preventive way and allow more open access services and more opportunity for families to refer themselves.

Management structures had sometimes been changed to save money. For example, in one centre, staffing had been reduced from one manager and one deputy per centre, to one manager for several centres. One potential benefit reported in these circumstances was that the family centres were working more closely together, ensuring a consistency of approach, which could be appropriate in areas of comparable need.

Explanations for the changing picture

We have provided above an overview of family centre service activity, including information about the changing nature of services and access to them. We now turn to trying to make sense of why these changes have taken place. We can identify four sets of issues which have clearly had a substantial impact on family centres over the last few years. These are:

- new policy directions
- funding
- multi-agency working
- the impact of Sure Start.

Changes associated with policy

The pace and scale of legislative change since 1997 was evident. New policies and initiatives were found to exert a very considerable influence on family centre work and their range of service provision. These new initiatives included Heath Action Zones, Single Regeneration Budget and Sure Start Local Programmes, Quality Protects, Best Value, the Framework for the Assessment of Children in Need and their Families, Ofsted, Children in Need Audit, and the emerging Community Safety Agenda.

Changes associated with funding

As suggested earlier, service changes did not simply occur in response to family centres' identification of changing needs, but were more likely to be driven by funding. This was true whether changes were service developments, changes in specialization, an increasing focus on core responsibilities, a move to rebalancing safeguarding and promoting welfare activities, or were cuts and closures or reductions in staff.

The changing nature of services was outlined earlier in Tables 9.1–9.3. There is evidence from the study which shows that, in part, family centres were changing to respond to funders' evolving requirements:

> We now get more money for the centre being used for contact arrangements supervised by the local authority and also for heavy child protection assessments mostly required by the court.

> There is new funding for service level agreements but not for neighbourhood services. The majority of work required is assessment/child protection focused – statutory services.

At review, two out of five (41%) family centres reported changes to their funding arrangements. A wide range of funding-related changes was reported, likely to be indicative of individual strategies adopted by funders. The biggest impact was on the voluntary sector and the ultimate change was the final closure of some family centres:

> We are directly affected by the county council's funding crisis and their need to concentrate funding on their core business i.e. child protection and we will close in the next few months.

At the point of our review survey, we found that, since the national survey:

- at least 6 per cent of family centres in the national survey had closed; this comprised 4 per cent of local authority and 10 per cent of non-local authority family centres

- four per cent of family centres in the national survey, all of them local authority, were no longer functioning as family centres

- one per cent of family centres in the follow-up survey were due to close imminently

- around 4 per cent of family centres in the follow-up survey reported that they were uncertain about funding.

In the review survey, we found some family centres were in dire financial straits, with large proportions of their funding having already been, or about to be, cut:

> Eighteen months ago we were threatened with closure because of the limited council budget. Budget reduced each year by top slicing before receiving funding – this year we have lost 5 per cent.

There were also comments from centre managers and staff that the increasing complexity of funding arrangements brought very heavy administrative demands. This could mean that services without extensive administrative support would have insufficient time or would lack the ability necessary to locate sources of funding and to make bids:

> Due to funding constraints on our budget we have to look for funding from other sources to keep all our services going. We find this very time-consuming and it takes time away from our users. We would like our funding restored. We have been very successful in obtaining funding from local charities, building societies, banks etc. for the last three years but it gets more and more difficult to approach people as time goes on.

> Grant for service provision was withdrawn by the local authority; therefore we spend an increased amount of time looking for other funding sources e.g. the national lottery – not always successfully! Services have been withdrawn and we have made a reduction of staff due to lack of funding. We were only able to offer services to fathers for a short time due to Home Office funding which has now come to an end.

> Funding arrangements are becoming more complex and the expertise required to write funding bids and fill in complicated returns for different funding sources has also become more complex. The project is expanding and taking on new bits of work with new sources of funding as new money and opportunities present themselves.

> Funding takes up an eternity each year.

Changes associated with multi-agency working

Some changes were related to multi-disciplinary and multi-agency working. Influenced by the implementation of the *Framework for the Assessment of Children in Need and their Families* (Department of Health *et al.* 2000), family centres were beginning to contribute to joint assessments with social workers. There was evidence that they were beginning to expand their range of services linked to health and education, such as pre-natal services in association with midwives; and to school inclusion work in primary schools. Family centres were also increasing the range of services by acting as a venue for other professionals and agencies, such as counselling and advice services.

Developments and issues within local authority social services were reported as negatively affecting family centre work. For example, shortages of mainstream social workers within local authority departments were influencing the work of family centres in that such shortages reduced the time that social workers had to plan and refer families to family centres. This was particularly disadvantaging families who might benefit from early intervention. Social workers in local authorities were preoccupied with crisis work:

> Due to staffing issues in social work teams, there has been an increase in child protection and unallocated child protection cases in social work teams. It feels like our staff hold more complex cases due to shortage of social work staff. My staff are despondent that their preventive work has been reduced.

There were reports of mainstream social workers under-valuing, under-using or wrongly using family centre services, through a lack of understanding of the centres' work. This was seen by centre staff as a further by-product of a rapid turnover of staff in social work teams, and of inexperienced social workers, who were under stress and not totally confident as to how to work with families. There were also reports of discrepant requirements at different levels within social services:

> Management are requesting more short session assessments, less family support, social inclusion work but this is not being requested by social workers. We feel the social workers still want to work directly and on a longer-term basis with families who need them.

In the review survey, there were various references to actual or potential changes in multi-agency working, particularly with education services, but also in respect of working with children's pediatric services, mental health services, family therapy services, the police, and youth offending services. We found evidence of an ongoing debate about who should be undertaking different roles and providing services. There was also much discussion about the relationship between funding policies and their impact on the joining up of services. The latter was particularly important as joint agency work or working from shared sites could sometimes represent a means to conserve or expand early intervention work. One example was work around school exclusion in primary schools.

Changes associated with the impact of Sure Start

Sure Start has the highest profile of all the area-based initiatives introduced by New Labour and it is the most likely to have had an impact on the work of family centres. The study found that family centres varied in their relationships with Sure Start. Sure Start local programmes were developing in the catchment area of almost half of the family centres in the follow up survey and were planned in a further 6 per cent. Just under two thirds of family centres located in Sure Start areas reported little or no impact on their centres, commenting that it was 'early days' or making similar references to the lengthy process of launching programmes.

There was a range of attitudes expressed towards Sure Start. Just over two fifths of family centres located in areas where Sure Start programmes were being implemented had positive views of the programme. However, the imbalance in resources between Sure Start and other family support agencies was a recurring theme which was seen as a matter of serious concern:

> Sure Start is just outside the area in which our family centre is situated. I feel there is a huge imbalance in resources which affects what we can do with 3.5 FTEs compared to Sure Start and their vast capital.

> We are really concerned that Sure Start has all the money at the expense of social services. This means we can have a far higher number of staff and deliver, without even thinking about it, all the things we have wanted to do over the years but have lacked the resources to put in place.

Although there could be negative outcomes for some family centres, in others, there were also felt to be perceptible gains in terms of funding for additional staff, services and resources. These variations in the actual impact of Sure Start on family centres can be explored under the following headings:

- collective approach to services
- funding
- resources for families, professionals and agencies
- preventive work
- numbers of families served
- service range
- negative aspects of Sure Start.

COLLECTIVE APPROACH TO SERVICES

A third of the family centres where Sure Start was reported to be having an impact referred to an increase in links, liaison and a collective approach to services. Actual or potential integration of services and staff was reported, in terms of joint work and mutual referrals, particularly when family centres acted as a base for the Sure Start local programme.

Family centres could be lead or co-ordinating agencies in Sure Start local programmes or be closely involved in the consultation process. Potential positive outcomes of links with Sure Start included taking the stigma away from social services through association with the Sure Start local programme, and the likelihood of additional referrals through contact with a wider range of potential referrers. There were references to consultation about families' problems and services, to decide who could provide the most appropriate services, how the duplication of services could be avoided, and in relation to the provision of commissioned services.

FUNDING

Twenty-two per cent of family centres who reported an impact as a result of Sure Start, referred positively to additional funding being available through the initiative. A minority of family centres referred to increased sustainability as a result of having an involvement in the programme. Four centres reported that they had been integrated into the Sure Start local programme. Local authority family centres were far less likely (8%) than independent/voluntary sector family centres (48%) to report an impact on funding.

However, Sure Start could also lead to a negative change in the focus of service provision. Time-limited funding associated with Sure Start (and other initiatives) could be a major concern, particularly in the context of other funding also being time-limited. Both of these could lead to the reduction or, as had happened in one case, the untimely ending of services.

RESOURCES FOR FAMILIES, PROFESSIONALS AND AGENCIES

Just under one third of family centres, where Sure Start was reported to be having an impact, referred to an increase in resources for families, professionals and agencies, including the family centres themselves. This was generally through centres becoming directly involved in the programme. Only four centres reported a decrease in resources.

Family centre workers as well as families were seen to benefit from additional resources, which could include additional in-house services such as teaching English as a second language; rapid access to a range of other professionals and services such as free interpreting services; additional equipment such as a toy library or a computer suite. Changes to premises were mentioned by 11 per cent of family centres where the programme was reported to be having an impact. There could be new buildings or improvements to existing buildings, such as playrooms, nurseries, offices, libraries and learning facilities.

Other developments in resources included additional staff and training, and the development of opportunities for staff. For example, one family centre reported the addition of a practitioner research team which had improved practice in the area of parents' involvement in children's learning and children's well-being.

PREVENTIVE WORK

Eleven per cent of family centres, where Sure Start was reported to be having an impact, referred to an increase in early intervention and preventive work, funding posts for specialist workers, such as those in early years services and general family support, so that these types of services could continue alongside child protection work. The more 'universal' approach adopted by Sure Start had enhanced the focus on early intervention work and could pre-empt the need for late intervention crisis work and statutory input.

NUMBERS OF FAMILIES SERVED

Nine per cent of family centres said that the impact of Sure Start was related to an increase in the number of families served and only 5 per cent to a decrease. Conversely, some family centres were experiencing reductions in referrals in general, and specifically, in terms of children under four years of age. Three family centres reported that Sure Start was obliging them to restrict their services to children over four years. Services for young children could be transferred to Sure Start, possibly with the exception of child protection work and work with looked-after children.

SERVICE RANGE

Seventeen per cent of family centres told us that Sure Start was helping an increase in their range of services but 5 per cent said their range of services had contracted. Overall, Sure Start was seen to have a significant impact on services to families both quantitatively and qualitatively.

Family centres in Sure Start local programmes areas were increasingly acting as 'one stop shops', providing a range of services to local families. Developments to family centre work included specific services and activities associated with Sure Start, such as family literacy and parent education; priority places on support groups for pregnant teenagers and teenage parents; a play-start service to parents and children under four; and services for fathers.

NEGATIVE ASPECTS OF SURE START

In spite of the substantial gains from Sure Start, a major concern, shared by many of the family centres, was that Sure Start operated in restricted geographical areas, which gave rise to 'have and have not families' often in adjacent communities, who had similar levels of need but different access to support. This concern increased when families from both groups attended the same family centre. Eligibility for services could then be based on postal address, not need:

> Sure Start area is only one seventh of our working area – therefore 'have' and 'have nots' is very marked.

> Sure Start is missing our identified areas of deprivation as we are not in an area of political deprivation. All government initiatives – Sure Start, Neighbourhood Nurseries, New Opportunities fund are all aimed at the same political wards or at working parents. There are still gaps for housing estates in semi-affluent areas.

Pointers to the future

In summary, it might be argued that the experiences of family centres over the period of this study provide a helpful reminder of the intended and unintended consequences of government policies for children and families, some of which are positive, some less so. In particular our findings paint a detailed picture of the ways in which one part of the child care workforce, the staff of family centres, has stayed abreast of the key policy developments which have emerged in the last five years, and has sought to maintain a continuum of accessible services for children and families. To do this, they have had to respond imaginatively throughout this period at both the strategic and the practice levels. The examples of good practice we have identified in both these spheres provide helpful insights into many of the components of the *Every Child Matters* agenda, in particular maximizing access to services; facilitating multi-agency working; and developing the workforce. Family centres, which have demonstrated a capacity for flexible and pro-active approaches to the needs of children and families in their communities could and should form a major building block in the new service system. They have a very considerable amount to offer.

What general lessons can be learned from the work of family centres over a very long period to implement the children's services agenda in the most effective way?

Policy makers need to be aware that their best intentions for increasing the quantity and quality of services for children and their families can have perverse and unintended consequences. Our study has illustrated this principle all too clearly in the form of the closure of some family centres. In other cases, family centres which once operated on a self referral, open access and universal basis have found their preventive services restricted to families whose children have been identified as being at risk of significant harm. Their opportunity to intervene in a preventive way to forestall more serious problems has been removed or, at the very least, circumscribed.

Careful thought needs to be given to the location of agencies who may share a similar purpose and role. For example, the impact of having several agencies with a similar 'preventive' brief, for example, in the current context, having family centres and Sure Start local programmes sited in the same area can mean that they end up competing for the same resources. This clearly can be counter-productive in a range of ways, including centres competing for the same funding and, in the context of a workforce shortage, vying for the same, limited number of available staff in a local area.

Where the funding of preventive agencies, including centre-based agencies is concerned, it needs to be recognized that the pursuit of diverse, complex and small pockets of funding is a time-consuming process which can reduce time available to deliver services.

All too often, these discrete sources of money lead to time-limited funding, which has a detrimental effect on forward planning and the continuity of services. Centre-based services need to be able to plan over a longer period, two or three years at the least, in order to maintain staff, to plan for the upkeep of their premises and to contribute to the local children's services planning process. Not to be able to do so leads to a vicious circle, whereby only guaranteeing short-term delivery of services will mean that they are not seen as serious partners by the local authority. For voluntary agencies, who have considerable credibility and experience in the area of preventive services, such short-term planning and funding can render a fatal blow to their survival. Beyond this, the exit of such agencies from the provision of children's centres will significantly reduce the range and diversity of services available to parents. This is ironic, to say the least, given the current emphasis placed by the Department for Education and Skills on the importance of parental choice.

It is a mistake to distinguish between children whose development is likely to be impaired and children 'at risk of significant harm'. They are all *children in need of services* under the Children Act 1989 (Department of Health 2001). Requiring some agencies to undertake very specific work, for example child protection assessments or work with looked-after children, imposes artificial barriers on the developmental needs of all children and risks losing the joint concept of simultaneously safeguarding and promoting the welfare of children.

It is important to recognize that many of the characteristics of services which parents find unhelpful and unattractive also reduce the job satisfaction of those who deliver services. Social work and social care staff are equally frustrated by finding their professional skills restricted to investigative work in the area of safeguarding. Given the fact that their motivation for joining the social work and social care workforce will have been led by an interest in improving outcomes for children and enhancing the quality of life for families, staff themselves resent the imposition of thresholds of eligibility. They find barriers between services inhibit their work in promoting the optimal development of children and the enhancement of parenting skills.

Finally, the most perverse form of rationing of services for children is one based on cut-off points according to children's chronological age. There are problems associated with strictly dividing up responsibility for delivering services to groups of children within different age bands. Such an approach neither takes account of individual developmental pathways nor the structure of families who have more than one child. Siblings are often likely to be affected by the problems of an identified child in need of services. Centre-based services must recognize that parents may be dealing simultaneously with children at different stages of development and be prepared to respond to their needs and preferences in relation to all their children. If they cannot meet a whole family's needs themselves, they need to know where their help can be supplemented and built upon by others.

In the last analysis, planners need to recognize that centre-based services represent a vital component in the overall network of services for children and families at the local level. Their ability to take account of all of the individual issues highlighted by families and staff in the study is only one half of the story. Centres possess the ability to ensure that the sum of the network is greater than its individual components. In other words, they provide a very tangible example of a combination of *working together* and *networking*. Given that these two approaches are central to current government aspirations for the shape of children's services, overlooking the potential contribution of family centres would seriously undermine the success of the *Every Child Matters* agenda. In short, family centres matter.

Family Centres: An Afterword

The previous chapters have drawn attention to the way in which, throughout the last four decades, the longstanding activities of family centres have anticipated almost all the themes in current policy and practice emphases of government. These themes include:

- an emphasis on preventive rather than reactive work
- partnership working
- multi-disciplinary working
- the mixed economy of child care provision
- the potential of commissioning and a trust-based approach
- a robust acknowledgement of the rights of those who use services to play a key role in the design and delivery of services.

The published record of these activities in a number of evaluations and studies has undoubtedly made a considerable, if largely unacknowledged, contribution to the knowledge base that underpins both *Every Child Matters* (CM 5860, 2003) and the ten-year strategy for child care (HM Treasury 2004).

The study reported in this book carries messages with a 'prospective' value for children's services, as well as providing a detailed retrospective account of family centres in the last decade. Taken together, the insights of managers, practitioners and those families who use family centres can help inform the implementation of the new systems and structures introduced in the agenda for change required by *Every Child Matters*.

Although we have entitled this final section 'an afterword', it is debatable whether this is a concept which can ever accurately be applied to family centres; their story will always be ongoing. Even as this book is being published, examples of the consistent, pro-active efforts which we have described throughout the book are still clearly in evidence. Family centre staff never sit back and rest on the previous policy agenda: they harness their capacity to move forward and capitalize on current and future policy potential. The current period well illustrates both the 'perversity' of the attitudes of central and local government to family centres, and at the same time, the capacity which family centres could, were they permitted, contribute to local service structures and networks. We provide current – that is, at the time of writing – examples of both these issues.

In 2005, the Family Centre Network, whose membership provided the sample for this study, was commissioned by the Department for Education and Skills to explore the likely impact of children's centres on family centres in England (Douglas 2005). Specifically, the Department for Education and Skills wanted to know how many family centres were moving towards becoming children's centres; and, if they were, how they could best be supported by local authorities. The survey results highlighted the very real danger that the knowledge and expertise, described at length in this book, will yet again be overlooked or at the very least not be exploited to the full. Approximately half the sample of family centres in the 2005 survey had not applied to become children's centres. One of the main reasons given for not doing so (by approximately one quarter of the sample) concerned their difficulty in providing the 'child care component' of the core offer, which government requires all children's centres to deliver (Department for Education and Skills July 2005).

Other centres explained that they lacked the available staff or resource to apply. These accounts echo the challenges we recorded in our own study around burdensome bidding processes for specific pots of often time-limited money. A smaller group of family centres were sceptical as to whether their existing resource levels would enable them to provide universal rather than referred services. However, a further dispiriting early finding from the Family Centre Network survey (Douglas 2005) was the fact that a significant number of centres, 40 per cent, had not been included in the National Child Care Strategy implementation consultations being undertaken by the local authority in which the centres were based. Only 17 per cent of voluntary sector sponsored family centres had been consulted.

As has been noted by the survey authors, no one really benefits from this apparent waste.

> The government's vision is of a 'children's centre in every community by 2008…' Family centres have an opportunity to capitalise on this, with their unique, holistic approach and centre based practice. On the other hand, Children's Centres may struggle to provide such a service, certainly from one site, which would continue to require funding alongside the rollout of Children's Centres and extended schools. (Douglas 2005, p.4)

In the same period as this survey, examples abound of the readiness and optimism with which family centres are, to the very best of their ability, embracing the new agenda for children and families. A centre manager, writing of local developments around the establishment of the local Children's Trust, explained that his centre was part of a core range of in-house services, and was in the process of building stronger links with education-based colleagues alongside existing relationships with health and social services. This manager highlighted both the fact that the stated intention of children's centres is to broaden into family support, and that the National Service Framework advocates family centres services. He and his colleagues in the family centre aspired to work alongside children's centres in an integrated way (Green 2005).

It would seem as though the current policy agenda raises two inter-related sets of key questions about the work of family centres in the next decade. The first group reflects tensions and debates which are far from new, indeed, which may be thought of as archetypal. The second group comprises more 'topical' strategic and operational dilemmas. Examples of the first set include:

- What should be the relationship between the needs and preferences of parents and the needs and preferences of children?

- What kind of balance should be struck between centre-based and outreach services?

- What should be the balance between universal and targeted services?

The second set are more clearly operational in nature and raise issues about the extent to which family centres can, are, and should be, prepared to make changes to their existing style of service delivery. For example, as Green (2005) indicates, in the last two or three years, some family centres with close ties to Sure Start local programmes have aligned themselves with the new agenda, and are hoping to be designated as children's centres. Their intention is to maintain the balance between day care and family support in equal measure. At the same time, other family centres are either excluded from this process by their local statutory agencies or find themselves unable to meet the core offer.

There is a real risk for those family centres who do not respond to the required day care core offer, of becoming regarded as stigmatizing, given that their service users will be parents not in employment, because they cannot find jobs, or have chosen not to work. The government's longstanding emphasis on return to work as a way out of poverty, reflected in the ten-year strategy for child care, produced by the Treasury and other departments (HM Treasury 2004), combined with the extension of the catchment areas in which parents are entitled to access day care, is highly likely to push the socio-economic characteristics of parents using the centres towards the more affluent.

There is already some suggestion in data presented by the National Evaluation of Sure Start Local Programmes (Melhuish *et al.* 2005; Tunstill *et al.* 2005) that the most vulnerable families may be deterred from using children's centres if they perceive a critical mass of more affluent, assertive and confident parents to be dominating the use of services. The Children's Centres Guidance, in calling for more assertive and imaginative efforts to engage the most vulnerable families successfully, also reflects government aspirations for local authorities to have a clearer idea of which families are, or are not, using the resources on offer (Department for Education and Skills December 2005).

The challenges faced by family centres in the next five years are, it could be argued, greater than at any time in their diverse existence. On the one hand, government is clearly committed to undertaking and achieving two inter-related tasks:

- maximizing *child development* along the *Every Child Matters* five key dimensions

- *supporting families* in a range of practical ways, including financial support, parenting support and targeted help, but deploying compulsion, such as parenting orders, if the former child development objectives are not achieved and where parents fail to take up services on a voluntary basis.

In 2005, on the basis of the findings we describe in this book, family centres are clearly in a pole position to 'hold the ring' between these two, potentially opposed approaches. They possess sought-after knowledge about the needs and preferences of parents; they have experience of the tasks involved in constructing local service networks; and they possess skills in joint working. These skills and knowledge need to be deployed to support the likelihood of local services meeting the needs of children and their parents.

We hope that the account we have presented will encourage local authorities to draw on the expertise and diverse, high-quality service provision of the centres located in their midst, and to strive towards creating in respect of children's centres the same level of credibility, respect and affection in which family centres are held by their local communities.

The Design, Collection and Analysis of the Data

It is helpful to understand both why and how this study was undertaken. The previous chapters have demonstrated why, in 1998, a study of family centres was a very timely undertaking. The Parenting Initiative research studies were commissioned by the previous Conservative government over a four-year period starting in 1996. This study was the only one of these to look at a specific area of family support, and its starting point was the then prominent role of family centres within a range of formal and informal support networks for parents and children. In particular, the study hoped to explore the viability of the Audit Commission's aspirations that family centres should become a 'one stop shop' for families to access family support services (Audit Commission 1994).

The study aims were as follows:

- to examine the potential of family centres to act as a gateway to family support services

- to explore the extent to which family centres facilitate or develop links with informal support networks within the community

- to identify the potential for family centres to act as co-ordinating centres for family support services.

Defining our terminology

We defined the links that family centres had with others in three main ways:

1. Service partnerships

This is where there were strong links between the centre and other agencies whereby services could be provided by the centre:

(a) in collaboration with another agency

(b) where the centre had been commissioned by another agency.

2. Informal links
This is where there were informal links between individual family centre workers and individual workers and resources in the community.

3. Formal links
These were links made by family centre workers on behalf of individual families in order to access service delivery beyond the centre. These links could emanate from individual circumstances or in the context of the networking policy of the family centre.

Within these three sets of linkages, there were a range of different stakeholders. These are outlined in Table A.1.

Table A.1 Stakeholders in family centres' links

Service partnerships	Informal links	Formal links
Health visitors	Church	GPs
Other health services	Community groups	Health visitors
Schools	Family	Other health services
Education services	Friends	Schools
Social services	Neighbours	Education services
Other public sector professionals and agencies	Other	Social services
Voluntary agencies		Other public sector professionals and agencies
Youth services		Voluntary agencies
Other		

We also asked about family centres' involvement in current government initiatives, for example, Early Excellence Centres; Early Years Development and Child Care; Education Action Zones; Health Action Zones; Healthy Living Programmes; New Deal for Communities; Out of School New Opportunities; Quality Protects; Single Regeneration; Sure Start. Where appropriate, these are referred to by name throughout the study.

Studying different perspectives
In order to examine fully the extent to which family centres had a linking and co-ordinating role, this study was designed to incorporate the perspectives of:

- family centre managers and workers
- parents who had experience of attending family centres
- workers from other agencies who had links with family centres.

Data analysis

Throughout the study, we used statistical programmes, primarily the Statistical Package for the Social Sciences, SPSS, to analyse the quantitative data. Qualitative data, derived from the semi-structured interviews with individuals and publicity and organizational data sources, was thematically analysed, focusing mainly on family centres' roles, objectives, philosophy and principles of work.

Three phases to the study

There were three phases to the study:

- **Phase 1**: a survey of an extensive sample of 559 family centres in England, in order to provide a baseline for the analysis of service delivery activity and organizational characteristics. (This is referred to throughout the book as *the national survey.*) This produced a response rate of 74 per cent i.e. 415 of our initial 559 centres contacted. There were various reasons why the rest did not participate. In 82 cases, family centres declined to take part. In six cases, the family centre had integrated with another service, and a further 28 centres were no longer operating as a family centre. Twenty-eight forms were returned marked 'gone away'.

- **Phase 2**: an in-depth study of a purposive sample of 40 family centres, selected from the extensive sample in order to examine specific aspects of family centre work. (This is referred to throughout the book as *the intensive study.*)

- **Phase 3**: a follow-up survey of respondents in the extensive sample of centres in order to provide an update on the issues arising from the data collected in Phase 2. (This is referred to throughout the book as *the review survey.*) By the time of this review survey, only 408 centres were still operating and of this number, 344 centres participated (a response rate of 84%).

Taken together, data from each element of the study provides an overview of the experience of family centres over a five-year period. The following diagram provides a resumé of the numbers participating in each of the three phases of the study.

Phase 1	Phase 2	Phase 3
1. The national survey	2. The intensive study	3. The review survey
National postal survey of 415 centres.	In-depth study in 38 centres of the views of managers, parents and staff from other agencies with whom family centres worked.	A follow-up survey of 408 centres still operating who had responded to the national survey. This produced data on 344 centres.

A detailed account of the three phases

Phase 1: a national survey of family centres

The extensive sample was based on membership of the Family Centre Network, associated with the National Council of Voluntary Child Care Organisations (NCVCCO).

At the beginning of 1999, the NCVCCO list of subscribers to the Family Centre Network was used as a basis for a postal survey of 559 family centres in England. The questionnaire comprised three sections:

- information about the organization of the family centre

- information about the family centre's involvement in government and other initiatives

- information about the function of the family centre.

In April 1999, non-responders were contacted by telephone, using the same questionnaire format, and in July 1999, a postal reminder was sent, with the result that 77 sets of data were obtained by telephone, and a further 338 by post.

Phase 2: an in-depth investigation of family centre work

A subset of 40 family centres was selected from the survey sample for more intensive study. The intensive sample were purposively selected to include family centres which were:

- based in the North, Midlands, South and London

- in rural and urban settings

- covering large and small catchment areas

- operating as part of local authority provision or as part of the independent/voluntary sector

- providing broad and narrow ranges of services

- having broad and narrow ranges of links with other sources of family support.

Data were gathered through:

1. **Interviews with managers** in family centres to discuss their views and experience of family centre work in the context of the aims of the study.

2. **Interviews with parents** who were or had recently been attending one of the 38 family centres in the intensive study sample. We sought their views on the position of the family centre in their own family support systems; and we looked at their needs and the services they received.

3. **A contacts survey using postal questionnaires** to a range of external stakeholders who had links with the family centres in the intensive study sample. We sought their views on the position of family centres in the family support network and the role of family centres as a gateway to services.

INTERVIEWS WITH MANAGERS

A total of 41 manager interviews was carried out, in 40 family centres. Nineteen of these centres were located in the North and Midlands and 21 in the South of England, including seven in London.

Family centre managers were, in general, keen to participate, with only two refusals. In two family centres the managers had left and not been replaced and no one else felt able to contribute. One interview was cancelled because of time constraints; and another because of the manager's personal circumstances.

We used a semi-structured interview schedule to collect in-depth, qualitative data on the interviewee's experience and views about their family centre's linking and co-ordinating roles. We also asked about their position within their local family support network. We encouraged them to summarize this data in a 'sociogram', which recorded, in a graphical form, their links to other sources of family support.

The aims of the study were explained to interviewees and they were then invited to discuss their work, with prompts and questions from the schedule when appropriate. Key question areas included the family centre's role as a gateway to services and the capacity of family centres to co-ordinate formal and informal family support services.

INTERVIEWS WITH PARENTS

Interviews were carried out with 83 parents/carers in 28 family centres, including three parents in a residential family centre.

To observe ethical guidelines and, in particular, to maintain the anonymity of parents until they had opted into the study, we asked the family centres to act as intermediaries on our behalf. Parents were given a friendly letter explaining the aims of the study and inviting them to participate. The final sample included a wide range of parents, whose reasons for attending family centres were diverse.

Sixteen interviews, although arranged, did not take place. (The weather conditions at that time were atypical with hurricane level winds and intensive storms.) In the main, parents notified us that they were unable to attend, due to circumstances such as the illness of their children, a need to attend a more pressing appointment, or difficulties with travel. One parent was interviewed with the help of an interpreter; another parent with learning difficulties attended with a support worker.

There were three sets of interviews carried out by the research team:

- 32 interviews at eleven family centres in the North and Midlands

- 32 interviews in ten family centres in London and the South

- 19 interviews in seven family centres in London and the South.

THE CONTACTS SURVEY USING POSTAL QUESTIONNAIRES TO GATHER THE VIEWS OF WORKERS FROM OTHER AGENCIES

Twenty-five of the 40 family centres in the intensive study sample provided names and addresses of additional contacts who would be in a position to comment on the work of the family centres. One hundred and forty-two questionnaires were issued to these external stakeholders of which 112 were returned (a response rate of 79%).

The final sample included a wide range of stakeholders and reflected a wide range of agencies and individuals with whom the family centres were in contact.

SUPPLEMENTARY DATA

To maximize the range of information, local social services departments were approached for relevant published information about family centre services. Departments responsible for the provision of services to children and families were asked to provide copies of their Children's Services plans and other information regarding policies and guidelines for family centres in their area.

About half of the local authorities responded. The information that was supplied rarely referred directly to family centre services, although one local authority usefully provided a copy of their review of family centre services in their area.

Phase 3: the review survey

In view of the scale and speed of some of the policy changes which we have described in Chapter 1, the research team took the decision to undertake a further review survey to ascertain what was happening to family centres two years after the study started. We had become aware through our fieldwork contacts that the scale of policy change, described in Chapter 1, had clearly begun to impact on family centres. We did not want to miss the opportunity of capturing some of the issues this raised for them.

We therefore designed and distributed a final survey questionnaire. This was issued to 408 family centres in the national survey who, we believed, at that stage, were still in operation. The remaining seven had closed. There were 344 responses. The review survey offered an opportunity to explore further issues arising from Phase 2 of the study. The review questionnaire was designed to provide an update on the issues arising from the data collected in Phase 2 as well as to capture the views of providers of family centre services on the impact on their work of the national policy changes.

The data collected provides a fascinating picture of the organization, provision and networking activity of family centres across the period between 1999 and 2003. Chapters 3 to 9 have described the findings. These findings reflect the optimal timing of this study for identifying the impact of New Labour policies on both children and families, as well as on the work of family centres and the lessons they enshrine for future policy and practice.

References

Adamson, J. (1987) 'Family centres.' In G. Horobin (ed.) *Why Day Care? Research Highlights in Social Work 14.* London: Jessica Kingsley Publishers.

Aldgate, J. and Bradley, M. (1999) *Supporting Families through Short Term Fostering.* London: The Stationery Office.

Aldgate, J. and Tunstill, J. (1995) *Making Sense of Section 17: Implementing Services for Children in Need.* London: Her Majesty's Stationery Office.

Atherton, C. (1987) *Residential Resources for Children.* London: Family Rights Group.

Audit Commission (1994) *Seen but not Heard. Developing Co-ordinating Community Child Health and Social Services for Children in Need.* London: Her Majesty's Stationery Office.

Auspos, P. and Kubisch, A. C. (2004) *Building Knowledge about Community Change: Moving Beyond Evaluations.* New York: The Aspen Institute.

Bachmann, M., Reading, R., Husbands, C., O'Brien, M., Thoburn, J., Shemilt, I., Watson, J., Jones, N., Haynes, R., Mugford, M. and the NECT team (in press) 'What are children's trusts? Early findings from a national survey.' *Child: Care, Health and Development.*

Balloch, H. and Taylor, M. (2001) *Partnership Working: Policy and Practice.* Bristol: The Policy Press.

Butt, J. and Box, L. (1998) *Family Centred: A Study of the Use of Family Centres by Black Families.* London: Racial Equality Unit.

Cannan, C. (1986) 'Sanctuary or stigma?' *Community Care.* 22 May, pp.14–17.

Cannan, C. (1992) *Changing Families: Changing Welfare.* Hemel Hempstead: Harvester Wheatsheaf.

Children's Workforce Development Council (2005) *What is the Children's Workforce Network?* Leeds: CWDC. Available from www.cwd.council.org.uk/aboutcwdc.childrensworkforce network.htm. Accessed May 2005.

Children's Workforce Network (2005) *What is the Children's Workforce Network?* Leeds: CWDC. Available from www.childrensworkforce.org.uk. Accessed May 2005.

Cigno, K. (1988) 'Consumer views of a family centre drop-in.' *British Journal of Social Work 18,* pp.361–375.

CM 5730 (2003) *The Victoria Climbié Inquiry. Report of an Inquiry by Lord Laming.* London: The Stationery Office.

CM 5860 (2003) *Every Child Matters.* London: The Stationery Office.

Colton, M., Dounz, C. and Williams, M. (1995) *Children in Need.* Aldershot: Avebury.

Coote, A., Allen, J. and Woodhead, D. (2004) *Finding Out What Works: Understanding Complex Community-based Initiatives.* London: The King's Fund.

Cox, A., Pound, A. and Puckering, C. (1992) 'Newpin. A befriending scheme and the therapeutic network for carers of young children.' In J. Gibbons (ed.) *The Children Act 1989 and Family Support: Principles into Practice.* London: Her Majesty's Stationery Office.

Daines, R. (1989) *A Study of Partnership Relationships at the Fulford Family Centre.* Barkingside: Barnardo's.

Department for Education and Skills (2004a) *Every Child Matters: Change for Children.* London: Department for Education and Skills.

Department for Education and Skills (2004b) *Common Assessment Framework: A Consultation.* London: Department for Education and Skills.

Department for Education and Skills (2005) *Children's Workforce Strategy: A Strategy to Build a World-class Workforce for Children and Young People.* London: Department for Education and Skills.

Department for Education and Skills (July 2005) *A Sure Start Children's Centre for Every Community, Phase 2 Planning Guidance (2006–08).* www.surestart.gov.uk/improvingquality/guidance/practiceguidance

Department for Education and Skills (December 2005) *Sure Start Children's Centres: Practice Guidance.* http://www.surestart.gov.uk/publications/index.cfm?document=1500

Department of Health (1990) *Principles and Practice in Regulations and Guidance.* London: Her Majesty's Stationery Office.

Department of Health (1991) *The Children Act 1989. Guidance and Regulations, Vol. 2.* London: Her Majesty's Stationery Office.

Department of Health (1993) *Children Act Report 1992: A Report by the Secretaries of State for Health for England and for Wales on The Children Act 1989 in Pursuance of their Duties under Section 83(6) of the Act, CM2144.* London: Her Majesty's Stationery Office.

Department of Health (1995) *Child Protection: Messages from Research.* London: Her Majesty's Stationery Office.

Department of Health (1998) *Quality Protects – Framework for Action.* London: Department of Health.

Department of Health (2001) *The Children Act Now: Messages from Research.* London: The Stationery Office.

Department of Health, Social Services Inspectorate (1995) *Inspectorate Report on the Analysis of a Sample of English Children's Service Plans 1993/4.* London: Department of Health.

Department of Health, Social Services Inspectorate (1998) *Planning to Deliver: Inspection of Children's Services Planning.* London: The Stationery Office.

Department of Health and Social Security, Social Services Inspectorate (1988) *Family Centres – A Change of Name or a Change of Practice.* London: Her Majesty's Stationery Office.

Department of Health and Department for Education and Employment (1996) *Children's Services Planning Guidance.* London: Department of Health.

Department of Health, Department for Education and Skills and Home Office (2000) *Framework for the Assessment of Children in Need and their Families.* London: The Stationery Office.

Douglas, E. (2005) 'Children's Centres agenda-building on the experience of family centres.' *Outlook,* Issue 26, p.4.

Eisenstadt, N. (1983) 'Working with parents and the community: a study of two family centres.' Unpublished MSc thesis. Cranfield Institute of Technology.

Ghate, D., Shaw, C. and Neal, H. (2000) *Fathers and Family Centres: Engaging Fathers in Preventative Services.* York: Joseph Rowntree Foundation.

Gibbons, J. (ed.) (1992) *The Children Act 1989 and Family Support: Principles into Practice.* London: Her Majesty's Stationery Office.

Giller, H. (1993) *Children in Need: Definition, Management and Monitoring.* London: Her Majesty's Stationery Office.

Glass, N. (1999) 'Sure Start: the development of an early intervention programme for young children in the United Kingdom.' *Children and Society 13,* 4, 257–264.

Glendinning, C., Powell, M. and Rummery, K. (2002) *Partnerships, New Labour and the Governance of Welfare.* Bristol: The Policy Press.

Green, A. (2005) 'Family Centre Focus: what works for parents?' *Outlook,* Issue 26, pp.13–15.

Green, J. (2003) 'Concepts of child attachment.' Paper given at the President's Interdisciplinary Conference, Dartington Hall, 12–14 September, published in The Rt. Hon. Lord Justice Thorpe and J. Cadbury (eds) (2004) *Hearing the Children*. London: Jordans.

Hardiker, P., Exton, K. and Barker, M. (1991) 'The social policy contexts of prevention in child care.' *British Journal of Social Work 21*, 4, 341–359.

Hasler, J. (1984) *Family Centres – Different Expressions, Same Principles*. Occasional Paper 1. London: The Children's Society.

Heaton, K. and Sayer, J. (1992) *Community Development and Child Welfare*. London: Community Development Foundation.

Hendrick, S. (2003) *Child Welfare: Historical Dimensions, Contemporary Debate*. Bristol. The Policy Press.

HM Treasury (1998) *Comprehensive Spending Review: Cross Departmental Review of Provision for Children*. London: HM Treasury.

HM Treasury (1999) *Opportunity for All*. London: The Stationery Office.

HM Treasury (2004) *Choice for Parents, the Best Start for Children: A Ten Year Strategy for Childcare*. London: HM Treasury.

Holman, R. (1987) 'Family centres.' In S. Morgan and P. Righton (eds) *Child Care Concerns and Conflicts*. London: Hodder and Stoughton.

Holman, R. (1988) *Putting Families First: Prevention and Child Care – A Study of Prevention by Statutory and Voluntary Agencies*. Basingstoke: Macmillan.

Hudson, B. (2005) 'What's the plan? *Community Care*. 9 November, pp.36–37.

Meadows, P. and Garbers, C. (2004) *Improving the Employability of Parents in Sure Start Local Programmes*. London: Department for Education and Skills.

Melhuish, E., Belsky, J., Leyland, A. and the NESS Team (2005) *Early Impacts of Sure Start Local Programmes on Children and Families*. London: Department for Education and Skills.

National Family Centre Network (1987) *Statement of Aims and Objectives*. London: National Council for Voluntary Child Care Organisations (NCVCCO).

Pawson, R. (2004) 'Simple principles for the evaluation of complex programmes.' In *Research in Education: What Works? Conference Proceedings*. London: Department for Education and Skills.

Performance and Innovation Unit, HM Government (2002) *Developing Integrated Services for Young Children and their Families*. London: Performance and Innovation Unit.

Quinton, D. (2004) *Supporting Parents: Messages from Research*. London: Department for Education and Skills and Department of Health.

Ranson, S. and Rutledge, H. (2005) *The Role of Family Centres in Encouraging Learning and Understanding within Families*. York: Joseph Rowntree Foundation.

Robbins, D. (ed.) (1993) *Community Care: Findings from Department of Social Security Funded Research*. London: Her Majesty's Stationery Office.

Rose, W. (1992) 'Foreword.' In J. Gibbons (ed.) The Children Act 1989 and Family Support: Principles into Practice. London: Her Majesty's Stationery Office.

Sanderson, I. (2002) 'Is it "What Works" that matters? Evaluation and evidence-based policy making.' Inaugural lecture. Leeds: Leeds Metropolitan University.

Smith, T. (1996) *Family Centres and Bringing up Young Children*. London: Her Majesty's Stationery Office.

Solesbury, W. (2001) *Evidence Based Policy: Whence it Came and Where it's Going.'* UK Centre for Evidence Based Policy and Practice, Working Paper 1. London: Economic and Social Research Council (ESRC).

Thoburn, J. (2002) *Adoption and Permanence for Children who Cannot Live Safely with Relatives, Quality Protects Research Briefing*. London: Department of Health, Research in Practice, Making Research Count.

Tisdall, K., Wallace, J., McGregor, E., Millen, D. and Bell, A. (2005) *The Provision of Integrated Services by Family Centres and New Community Schools*. York: Joseph Rowntree Foundation.

Tunstill, J. (2002) 'Adoption and family support – two means in support of the same end.' In A. Douglas and T. Philpot (eds) *Adoption: Changing Families, Changing Times.* London: Routledge.

Tunstill, J., Aldgate, J., Wilson M. and Sutton, P. (1995) 'Crossing the organisational divide: family support services.' *Health and Social Care in the Community 4*, 1, 41–49.

Tunstill, J. and Aldgate, J. (2000) *Children in Need: From Policy to Practice.* London: The Stationery Office.

Tunstill, J., Allnock, D., Akhurst, S., Garbers, C. and the NESS Research Team (2005) 'Sure Start Local Programmes: implications of case study data from the National Evaluation of Sure Start.' *Children and Society 19*, 1–14.

University of East Anglia and National Children's Bureau (2005) *Realising Children's Trusts Arrangements: National Evaluation of Children's Trusts, Phase 1.* Norwich: University of East Anglia.

Warren, C. (1993) *Family Centres and the Children Act 1989. A Training and Development Handbook.* Brighton: University of Sussex/Department of Health.

Subject index

Author index